# Quick-to-Stitch
# Weekend
# Quilts & Projects™

Edited by Jeanne Stauffer and Sandra L. Hatch

HOUSE of
WHITE
BIRCHES
PUBLISHERS
SINCE 1947

# Quick-to-Stitch Weekend Quilts & Projects

Editors: Jeanne Stauffer, Sandra L. Hatch
Design Manager: Vicki Blizzard
Associate Editor: Barb Sprunger
Copy Editors: Mary Nowak, Sue Harvey, Nicki Lehman
Publication Coordinator: Tanya Turner

Photography: Tammy Christian, Jeff Chilcote, Justin P. Wiard
Photography Stylist: Arlou Wittwer
Photography Assistant: Linda Quinlan

Production Coordinator: Brenda Gallmeyer
Book Design: Erin Augsburger
Cover Design: Jessi Butler
Technical Artist: Connie Rand
Production Artist: Pam Gregory
Production Assistants: Janet Bowers, Marj Morgan
Traffic Coordinator: Sandra Beres

Publishers: Carl H. Muselman, Arthur K. Muselman
Chief Executive Officer: John Robinson
Marketing Director: Scott Moss
Book Marketing Manager: Craig Scott
Product Development Director: Vivian Rothe
Publishing Services Manager: Brenda Wendling

Printed in the United States of America
First Printing: 2001
Library of Congress Number: 00-109647
ISBN: 1-882138-72-4

# ❧ Quilt Notes ❧

People are so busy these days. Between working, taking care of a home and family, there isn't enough time to do the things you have to do, never mind doing something just for fun or because you want to.

If quilting is one of your favorite activities but time is a problem, you are in luck. We have collected projects for the quilter with a few free hours. These projects may be used as gifts, thereby serving a dual purpose, or they might be made just for the fun of it and as a gift for you.

For quilters working outside the home, evening and weekends are the only available time to get everything done. It might be hard to take a week of evenings or one whole weekend away from it all to quilt, but if you can do it, it will be worth your efforts!

Making a quilt or quilted project in 20 hours or less is a remarkable accomplishment. While some quilters may not be able to finish a project in this amount of time, we know that others will breeze right through. We are assuming you will do every step

by machine, but if you prefer to do hand-piecing, -appliqué and -quilting, that is fine. It might just take a little more time. The important thing is to savor the process and enjoy the time you spend quilting.

Have a wonderful time as you look through the entire book for the perfect project to begin this weekend. Try out a new method or technique in your favorite colors or go out on a limb and make something entirely different than your usual choices.

Whether you take a few hours, evenings or days, we know that you will enjoy and benefit from the time spent quilting. Just imagine the sense of real accomplishment you'll feel when you've completed your project!

We wish you many hours of enjoyable quilting as you make the projects in this book.

Happy quilting!

*Jeanne Stauffer*

*Sandra L. Hatch*

# ❧ Contents ❧

## 8-Hour Quilting

## The Christmas Home

# ✃Contents✃

## Quick Classics

## Glorious Bed Quilts

## General Instructions

# 8-Hour Quilting

*If you need a quilted gift for a friend or family member you are sure to find the perfect item in this chapter, and you can stitch it in only eight hours! Whether you need a garment, a decorator item or something more personal, this chapter is the place to begin.*

*If you can't devote eight continuous hours to your project, a couple of evenings will suffice.*

*While you are at it, make a sample of the same project to keep on hand for the next gift-giving occasion.*

# Quilter's Cosmetic & Sewing Bags

By Jill Reber

*Make an indispensable bag for your long-distance trips,
or even those short excursions to a quilting class.*

## Flying Geese Bag

| Project Specifications |
| --- |
| **Skill Level:** Beginner |
| **Project Size:** 8" x 10" |

| Materials |
| --- |
| • 4 strips dark blue 2 1/2" x 10 1/2" |
| • 10 blue rectangles 2 1/2" x 4 1/2" |
| • 20 cream squares 2 1/2" x 2 1/2" |
| • 2 rectangles lining fabric 8 1/2" x 10 1/2" |
| • 2 rectangles batting 8 1/2" x 10 1/2" |
| • Cream all-purpose thread |
| • 12" nylon zipper |
| • Basic sewing supplies and tools |

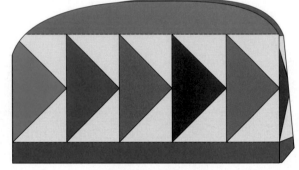

**Flying Geese Bag**
Placement Diagram
8" x 10"

## Instructions

**Step 1.** Lay one cream square on one blue rectangle; draw a line on the diagonal as shown in Figure 1. Sew on the marked line; trim seam to 1/4" as shown in Figure 2 and press.

**Figure 1**
Lay 1 cream square
on 1 blue rectangle;
draw a line on the
diagonal as shown.

**Figure 2**
Sew on the marked
line; trim seam to
1/4" as shown.

**Step 2.** Lay another cream square on the same blue rectangle; draw a line on the diagonal as shown in Figure 3. Sew, trim and press as in Step 1 to complete one Flying Geese unit as shown in Figure 4. Repeat for 10 Flying Geese units.

**Step 3.** Join five Flying Geese units to make a strip as shown in Figure 5; repeat for two strips. Press seams in one direction.

**Step 4.** Sew a 2 1/2" x 10 1/2" dark blue strip to opposite long sides of each strip as shown in Figure 6; press seams toward strips.

2 1/2" x 2 1/2"

**Figure 3**
Lay another cream
square on the same
blue rectangle; draw a
line on the diagonal.

**Figure 4**
Complete 1 Flying
Geese unit as shown.

**Figure 5**
Join 5 Flying Geese
units to make a strip.

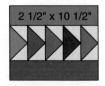

2 1/2" x 10 1/2"

**Figure 6**
Sew a 2 1/2" x 10 1/2" dark
blue strip to opposite long
sides of each strip.

**Step 5.** Sandwich a batting rectangle between a Flying Geese strip and one lining rectangle; pin or baste layers together to hold flat. Repeat for second strip.

**Step 6.** Quilt both sections as desired by hand or machine. ***Note:*** *The sample shown was machine-quilted in a straight line through the center of the Flying Geese strips and close to border strip seams using cream thread.*

**Step 7.** Prepare template for bag using pattern given.

**Step 8.** Cut quilted shapes to fit pattern. Edge-finish around each shape using a machine zigzag stitch or serger to secure raw edges.

**Step 9.** On one top edge with right sides together, sew zipper to bag. Align and repeat with other side. Stitch across nylon zipper to form a stop at each end as shown in Figure 7; trim off excess.

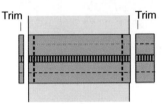

**Figure 7**
Stitch across nylon zipper to form
a stop at each end as shown.

**Step 10.** Unzip bag halfway; align three other sides and sew around using a 1/4" seam allowance.

**Step 11.** To form bottom of bag, fold ends together at one corner, matching open seams as shown in Figure 8; pin. Measure up 1 1/4" from folded point and mark a line as shown in Figure 9; sew on marked line. Tack corner to hold in place or trim seam to 1/4" and stitch on raw edge to finish seam. Repeat for second corner to finish. ➤

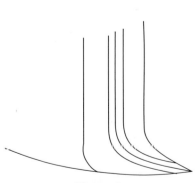

**Figure 8**
Fold ends together at 1 corner,
matching open seams.

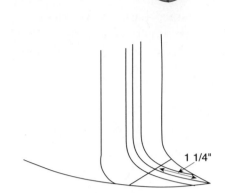

**Figure 9**
Measure up 1 1/4" from folded
point and mark a line as shown.

## Tulip Bag

| Project Specifications |
| --- |
| **Skill Level:** Beginner |
| **Project Size:** 8" x 10" |

| Materials |
| --- |
| • 2 rectangles blue sky fabric 8 1/2" x 10 1/2"<br>• Rectangle green print 3" x 10 1/2"<br>• Scraps green, orange, yellow and rose prints<br>• 2 rectangles lining fabric 8 1/2" x 10 1/2"<br>• 2 rectangles batting 8 1/2" x 10 1/2"<br>• All-purpose thread to match fabrics<br>• 1/4 yard fusible transfer web<br>• 12" nylon zipper<br>• Basic sewing supplies and tools |

**Tulip Bag**
Placement Diagram
8" x 10"

## Instructions

**Step 1.** Prepare patterns for appliqué shapes using patterns given. Trace shapes onto the paper side of the fusible transfer web referring to patterns for number to cut. Cut out shapes, leaving a margin around each one.

**Step 2.** Fuse paper shapes to the wrong side of fabric scraps referring to patterns for color. Cut out shapes on drawn lines; remove paper backing.

**Step 3.** Place the grass piece on one blue sky rectangle lining up bottom edge of grass with bottom edge of rectangle; fuse in place. Arrange three flower motifs on the grass and sky area referring to the Placement Diagram and photo of project for positioning suggestions; fuse in place.

**Step 4.** Sandwich a batting rectangle between the fused piece and one lining rectangle; pin or baste layers together to hold flat.

Sandwich the second batting rectangle between the remaining blue sky rectangle and lining rectangles; pin or baste layers together.

**Step 5.** Using all-purpose thread to match fabrics, machine-appliqué each shape in place, adding a satin-stitched stem referring to pattern.

**Step 6.** Finish bag as in Steps 7–11 for Flying Geese Bag. ❧

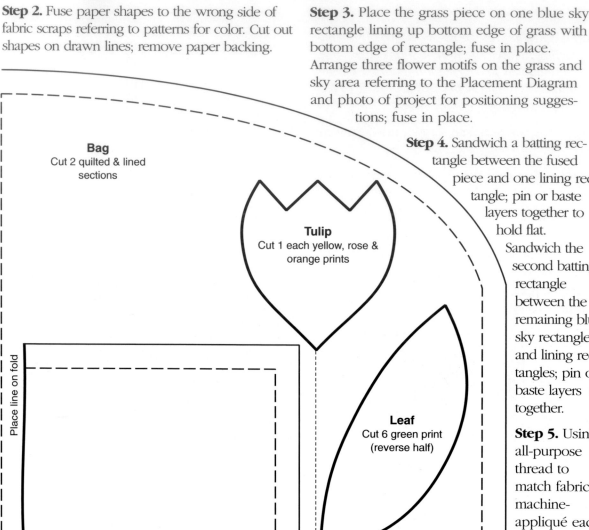

**Bag**
Cut 2 quilted & lined sections

**Tulip**
Cut 1 each yellow, rose & orange prints

**Leaf**
Cut 6 green print
(reverse half)

Place line on fold

**Grass**
Cut 1 green print

Place line on fold

# My Dog Is an Angel Sweatshirt

By Janice Loewenthal

*Dog lovers will enjoy making and wearing this redwork-design sweatshirt.*

### Materials

- Adult-size white sweatshirt
- 3/8 yard each 3 coordinating red prints in light, medium and dark values
- All-purpose thread to match fabrics
- Red all-purpose thread
- Red 6-strand embroidery floss
- 3/8 yard fusible transfer web
- 1/2 yard fabric stabilizer
- Basic sewing supplies and tools and water-erasable marker or pencil

## Instructions

**Step 1.** Prewash all fabrics and check embroidery floss for colorfastness. From dark red print, cut four strips 1 7/8" x 3 1/4" for A and eight squares 1 7/8" x 1 7/8" for B.

**Step 2.** From light red print, cut eight squares 1 7/8" x 1 7/8" for C and 16 squares 1" x 1" for D.

**Step 3.** To piece one corner heart block, place one light red print C square right sides together with A as shown in Figure 1; mark the diagonal of C and stitch on the marked line as shown in Figure 2.

**Figure 1**
To piece 1 corner heart block, place 1 light red print C square right sides together with A as shown.

**Figure 2**
Mark the diagonal of C and stitch on the marked line as shown.

**Step 4.** Trim seam allowance to 1/4" as shown in Figure 3. Repeat on opposite corner to complete bottom half of block as shown in Figure 4.

**Figure 3**
Trim seam allowance
to 1/4" as shown.

**Figure 4**
Repeat on opposite corner
to complete bottom half of
block as shown.

**Step 5.** Place one light red print D on one corner of a dark red print B. Mark, stitch and trim as in Steps 3 and 4 and referring to Figure 5; repeat on adjacent corner. Repeat for a second B-D unit.

**Step 6.** Join the A-C unit with the two B-D units to complete one Heart block as shown in Figure 6; repeat for four Heart blocks.

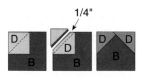

**Figure 5**
Mark, stitch and trim as shown.

**Figure 6**
Join the A-C unit with the 2
B-D units to complete 1
Heart block as shown.

**Step 7.** Cut one strip light red print 1 1/2" by fabric width and one strip each dark and medium red prints 1 1/4" by fabric width.

**Step 8.** Sew the light red print strip between the dark and medium red print strips; press seams toward darker fabrics. Cut strip set into four 11" segments. ***Note:*** *If fabric is not 44" wide, two strips of each color will be needed.*

**Step 9.** Sew a Heart block to each end of two 11" segments as shown in Figure 7; press seams toward strips. Join these two strips with the shorter strips to make an open square as shown in Figure 8; press seams toward strips.

**My Dog Is an Angel
Sweatshirt**
Placement Diagram
Size Varies

**Figure 7**
Sew a Heart block to each end of
two 11" segments as shown.

**Figure 8**
Join these 2 strips with the
shorter strips to make an
open square as shown.

**Step 10.** Cut two pieces each fusible transfer web 3" x 16 1/2" and 3" x 11". Fuse a piece to each corresponding side of the square; remove paper backing.

**Step 11.** Center and fuse open square on the front of the white adult-size sweatshirt referring to the Placement Diagram and photo of project for positioning.

**Step 12.** Place a piece of fabric stabilizer behind

the fused square. Using a medium-width machine satin stitch, sew around all raw edges to appliqué in place; remove fabric stabilizer.

**Step 13.** Using a water-erasable marker or pencil, transfer dog shape and letters to the center of the appliquéd open square referring to the Placement Diagram and photo of project for positioning.

**Step 14.** Using 3 strands of red embroidery floss, backstitch on marked lines for letters and dog shapes referring to Figure 9. Remove transfer lines referring to marker or pencil manufacturer's instructions. ❧

**Figure 9**
Backstitch as shown.

# Lovely Lotus Tote

By Judith Sandstrom

*This simple denim tote is sturdy enough to carry to the grocery store, library or quilting class.*

## Project Specifications

**Skill Level:** Beginner
**Project Size:** 16" x 12 3/4"

## Materials

- Scraps 3 red, 2 green and 1 yellow print
- 1/8 yard cream-on-cream print
- 1/2 yard denim
- Gray, light green, navy and cream all-purpose thread
- 2" piece 1/4"-wide light green satin ribbon
- 2" piece 1/4"-wide lightweight fusible adhesive
- 2 1/4 yards 7/8"-wide lightweight fusible adhesive
- 3 1/2 yards 7/8"-wide cream grosgrain ribbon
- Basic sewing supplies and tools and tracing paper

## Instructions

**Step 1.** Make one copy of each pattern given.

**Step 2.** Complete paper-piecing referring to Paper-Piecing Hints.

**Step 3.** Join the two pieced top sections as shown in Figure 1; press seams open. Join the two pieced bottoms sections again referring to Figure 1.

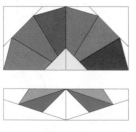

**Figure 1**
Join the 2 top sections; join
the 2 bottom sections.

**Step 4.** Iron the 2" piece lightweight fusible adhesive to the wrong side of the 2" piece of light green 1/4"-wide satin ribbon; remove paper backing.

**Step 5.** Center the ribbon over the seam line between the two pieced bottom sections as shown in Figure 2; fuse in place.

**Figure 2**
Center the ribbon over the seam line
between the 2 pieced bottom sections.

**Step 6.** Join the bottom pieced section with the top pieced section to complete the block as shown in Figure 3; press seams toward top section. Remove paper foundations.

**Step 7.** Cut a 17" x 28" rectangle denim; zigzag along both long edges to minimize fraying.

**Lovely Lotus Tote**
Placement Diagram
16" x 12 3/4"

**Figure 3**
Join the bottom pieced section with the
top pieced section to complete the block.

ends of the denim rectangle 3 1/2" from each
side and 1/4" from raw edge as shown in
Figure 4.

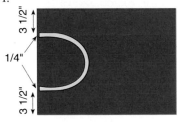

**Figure 4**
Baste straps 3 1/2" from each
side and 1/4" from the short
raw edge of the denim
rectangle.

**Step 8.** Cut the 7/8"-wide cream grosgrain ribbon as follows: two 5" lengths, two 8" lengths and four 24" lengths. Cut two of each size lengths 7/8"-wide lightweight fusible adhesive.

**Step 9.** Fuse lengths of fusible adhesive to corresponding-size lengths grosgrain ribbon; remove paper backing. Align the two remaining 24" lengths of grosgrain ribbon on the adhesive side of the two fused ribbon lengths; fuse the pieces together to make a thick, double layer for straps.

**Step 10.** Pin and baste the straps on the short

**Step 11.** Fold under short denim edge 1/4"; stitch close to the raw edge. Fold under same edge 1" and stitch. Pull the ribbon strips to the top and topstitch close to the top edge as shown in Figure 5. Stitch a square shape on the inside edge around ribbon area to further reinforce straps as shown in Figure 6; repeat on opposite end.

**Figure 5**
Pull the ribbon strips to the top and topstitch close to the top edge as shown.

**Figure 6**
Stitch a square shape on the inside edge around ribbon area to further reinforce straps as shown.

**Step 12.** Center the pieced block 3 3/4" from the top of one finished edge of the denim rectangle; pin in place. Place the 5" fused grosgrain ribbon lengths 1/4" over the side edges of the pieced block as shown in Figure 7; fuse in place.

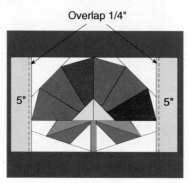

**Figure 7**
Place the 5" fused grosgrain ribbon lengths 1/4" over the side edges of the pieced block.

**Step 13.** Trim the 8" fused grosgrain ribbon lengths to the exact size of the previously fused section; fuse a length on the top and bottom as in Step 12.

**Step 14.** Using thread to match the grosgrain ribbon, zigzag-stitch around inside and outside edges of grosgrain-ribbon frame.

**Step 15.** Fold the denim rectangle in half with right sides together. Pin and stitch the side seams 1/2" from edge. Stitch again 1/4" from edge to reinforce seam. Turn the bag right side out; press to finish. ❧

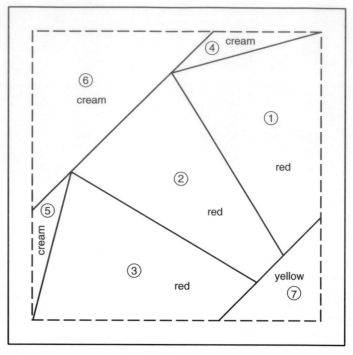

**Top Piece 1**

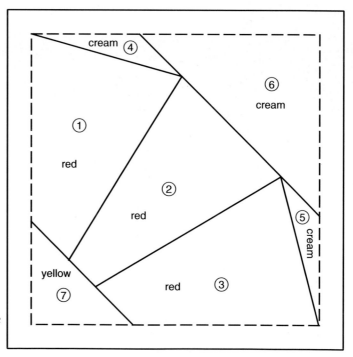

**Top Piece 2**

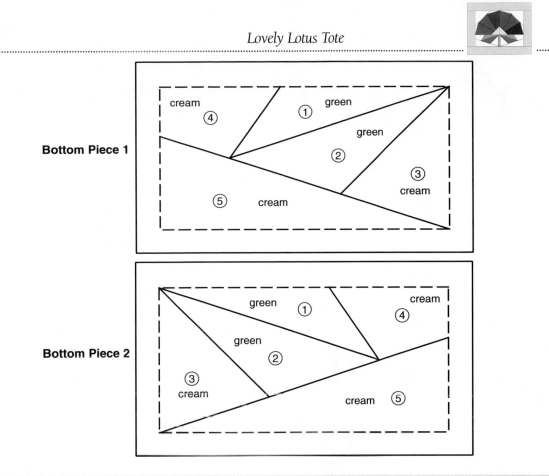

Bottom Piece 1

Bottom Piece 2

## Paper-Piecing Hints

Each paper foundation block has numbered sections. Add fabrics in numerical order, stitching on the line separating the two numbers.

Each piece of fabric must be large enough to cover the corresponding numbered space on the paper plus 1/4" or more outside the lines.

Hold the paper up to the light each time you add a piece of fabric to assure it is large enough.

The block is stitched on the printed side of the paper, but the fabric is placed on the unprinted side. Therefore, blocks which are not symmetrical will face in the direction opposite the paper foundation. Refer to the individual blocks for color placement.

**1.** Set sewing machine for 16–18 stitches per inch. Use a neutral gray-colored thread.

**2.** Place a piece of fabric for piece #1 right side up on the unprinted side of the paper foundation; pin in place.

**3.** Place the fabric for piece #2 right side down over piece #1; stitch along the line between pieces 1 and 2 on the marked side of the paper, beginning and ending two stitches beyond the actual stitching line.

**4.** Fold down the paper along the stitching line; trim seam allowance to 1/8"–1/4", taking care not to cut paper. Press the seam from the fabric side toward the last fabric added.

**5.** Repeat this procedure for all numbered pieces. Be sure pieces at the edge of the block extend beyond the outer dotted line.

**6.** Stitch around the outer edge of each completed block between the solid line and the dotted line. Cut on the solid line, removing excess fabric and paper edges.

**7.** Leave the paper foundation attached until all blocks are joined together. Some designs require more than one paper-pieced section to complete one block.

**8.** Use tweezers to remove the pieces of paper which have been perforated by the stitching.

# Sunflower Centerpiece

By Marian Shenk

*Make this bright centerpiece using four yellow prints in a Dresden-Plate design to resemble a sunflower.*

## Project Specifications

**Skill Level:** Beginner
**Project Size:** 24" x 24"

## Materials

- 1/4 yard each 3 yellow prints
- 1 square light yellow print 10" x 10"
- Backing 29" x 29"
- Batting 29" x 29"
- All-purpose thread to match fabrics
- Yellow quilting thread
- 3/4 yard 1"-wide white lace
- 3/4 yard 1/2"-wide gold braid
- Basic sewing supplies and tools

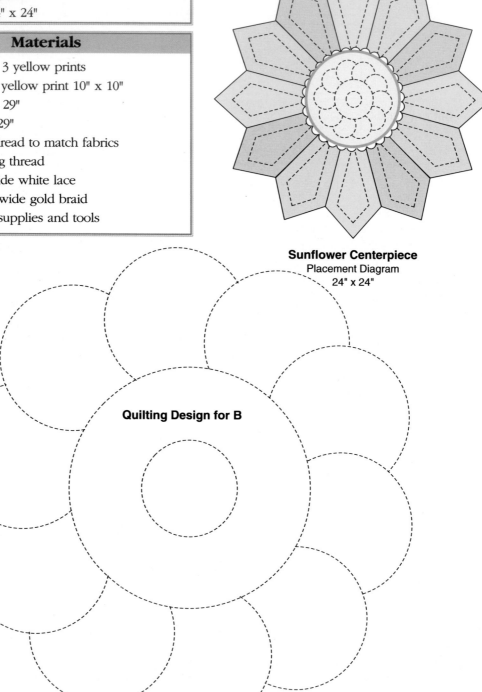

**Sunflower Centerpiece**
Placement Diagram
24" x 24"

**Quilting Design for B**

## Instructions

**Step 1.** Prepare templates using pattern pieces given; cut as directed on each piece.

**Step 2.** Join three different yellow print A pieces as shown in Figure 1; repeat with fabrics in the same order for four A sections.

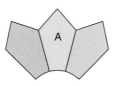

**Figure 1**
Join 3 different yellow print A pieces.

**Step 3.** Join the pieced A sections to complete a circle; press seams in one direction.

**Step 4.** Lay pieced section on a flat surface. Center the B circle piece on top to cover center hole; hand-baste in place to hold.

**Step 5.** Pin 1"-wide white lace around edges of circle, overlapping ends slightly; stitch in place.

**Step 6.** Cover stitching line with the gold braid, butting ends of braid; stitch through the center of the braid to attach.

**Step 7.** Lay batting on flat surface; lay the backing piece with wrong side on top of batting. Lay the pieced top right sides together with backing.

**Step 8.** Stitch all around pieced shape using a 1/4" seam allowance and leaving a 3" opening on one point; trim batting and backing even with pieced shape, clipping corners and points.

**Step 9.** Turn right side out through opening; hand-stitch opening closed.

**Step 10.** Mark quilting lines on A and B pieces referring to pattern and Placement Diagram for positioning. Hand-quilt on marked lines using yellow quilting thread to finish. ❧

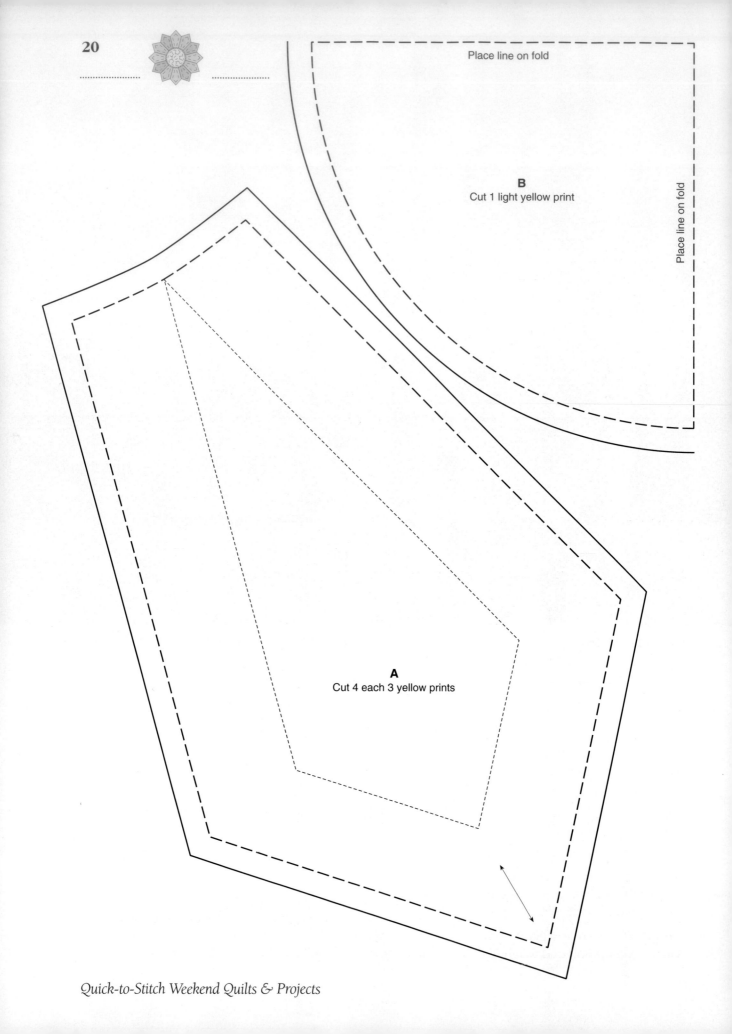

Place line on fold

Place line on fold

**B**
Cut 1 light yellow print

**A**
Cut 4 each 3 yellow prints

# Foundation-Pieced Fan Hot Pad

## By Kate Laucomer

*Foundation piecing makes stitching this complicated-looking fan-design hot pad a cinch.*

### Project Specifications

**Skill Level:** Intermediate

**Project Size:** 8" x 8" (includes binding)

### Materials

- Scrap dark blue print
- Scraps 7 different medium-to-dark blue prints
- Fat eighth white-on-white print
- Backing 9" x 9"
- Batting 9" x 9"
- 2" x 36" strip dark blue print for binding
- Neutral color all-purpose thread
- Basic sewing supplies and tools and tracing paper

### Instructions

**Step 1.** Transfer fan design to tracing paper using full-size pattern in Figure 1 on page 23; pattern is already reversed.

**Step 2.** Cut a piece to cover area 1 with excess being at least 1/4" larger all around; repeat for all pieces, referring to pattern piece for numbers and colors.

**Step 3.** Lay piece #1 on unmarked side of tracing paper pattern referring to lines as they show through as shown in Figure 2. ***Note:*** *Refer to the General Instructions and page 17 for more details about foundation piecing.*

**Step 4.** Pin piece #2 on piece #1; turn paper

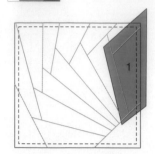

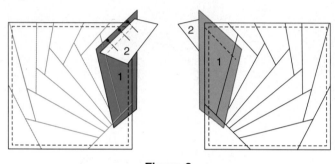

**Figure 2**
Lay piece #1 on unmarked
side of tracing paper pattern
referring to lines as they show
through as shown.

over and stitch on marked line as shown in
Figure 3.

**Figure 3**
Pin piece #2 on piece #1; turn paper over
and stitch on marked line as shown.

**Step 5.** Turn paper over again; trim excess to
1/8"–1/4" seam allowance. Press piece #2 flat
as shown in Figure 4.

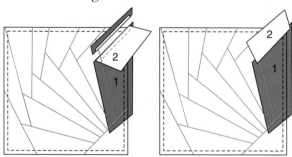

**Figure 4**
Trim excess to 1/8"–1/4" seam allowance.
Press piece #2 flat as shown.

**Step 6.** Continue adding pieces in numerical
order until entire paper is covered.

**Step 7.** Trim excess to paper edge, which
includes a 1/4" seam allowance; remove paper.

**Step 8.** Sandwich batting between pieced top
and backing square; pin or baste layers together.

**Step 9.** Outline-quilt fan shape using all-
purpose thread to match fabrics. When
quilting is complete, trim edges even; remove
pins or basting.

**Step 10.** Cut a 1" x 4" strip blue scrap. Fold
along length with right sides together; stitch.
Turn right side out through one end; press to
make hanging loop. Pin loop to one backside
corner of stitched piece as shown in Figure 5.

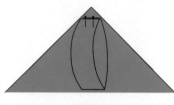

**Figure 5**
Pin loop to 1 backside corner
of stitched piece as shown.

**Step 11.** Bind edges with 2" x 36" dark
blue strip referring to the General
Instructions to finish. ❧

**Foundation-Pieced Fan Hot Pad**
Placement Diagram
8" x 8"
(includes binding)

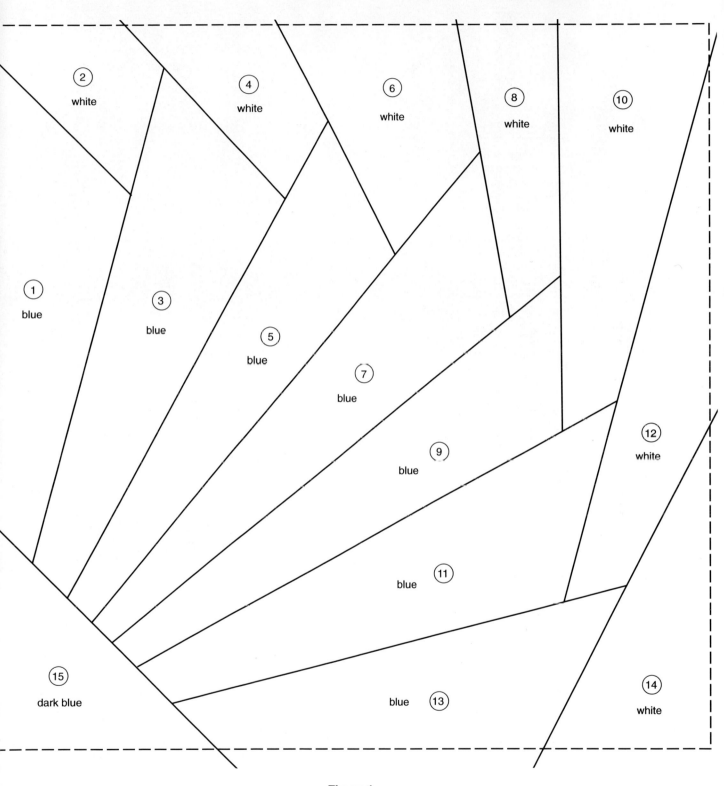

**Figure 1**
Trace this full-size pattern onto tracing paper.

# Tasseled Sofa Throw

By Carla Schwab

*Add tassels to an otherwise very simple throw to give an elegant but whimsical feeling to your sofa.*

## Project Specifications

**Skill Level:** Beginner

**Project Size:** Approximately 45" x 45"

## Materials

- 3/8 yard gold floral
- 1/2 yard green floral
- 7/8 yard burgundy plaid
- Backing 49" x 49"
- Batting 49" x 49"
- Neutral color all-purpose thread
- 8 or 16 tassels—gold, burgundy and green
- Basic sewing supplies and tools

## Instructions

**Step 1.** From gold floral, cut one 8" x 8" square for A and two 11 7/8" x 11 7/8" squares for B. Cut each B square in half on both diagonals to make B triangles. You will need four gold floral B triangles.

**Step 2.** From green floral, cut four 8" x 8" squares for A and four 8" x 11 1/2" rectangles for C.

**Step 3.** From burgundy plaid, cut two 11 7/8" x 11 7/8" squares for B. Cut each B square in half on both diagonals to make B triangles. You will need eight burgundy plaid B triangles. Cut two 11 1/2" x 11 1/2" squares for D. Cut each D square in half on one diagonal to make four burgundy plaid D triangles.

**Step 4.** Sew two gold floral B triangles to opposite sides of C, matching square ends as shown in Figure 1. Trim excess C using a straight-edge ruler to continue line of B as shown in Figure 2; repeat for two B-C units.

**Figure 1**
Sew 2 gold floral B triangles to opposite sides of C, matching square ends as shown.

**Figure 2**
Trim excess C using a straight-edge ruler to continue line of B as shown.

**Step 5.** Join the remaining C rectangles with A as shown in Figure 3.

**Step 6.** Join the A-C unit with the two B-C units as shown in Figure 4; trim excess C as in Step 4 and referring to Figure 5. Press seams toward darker fabrics.

**Step 7.** Sew a burgundy plaid B triangle to adjacent sides of a green floral A square as shown in Figure 6; press seams toward B. Repeat for four A-B units.

**Step 8.** Sew an A-B unit to each side of the A-B-C center section; press seams toward the A-B units.

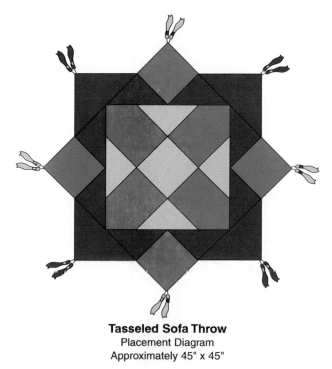

**Tasseled Sofa Throw**
Placement Diagram
Approximately 45" x 45"

**Figure 3**
Join the remaining C rectangles with A as shown.

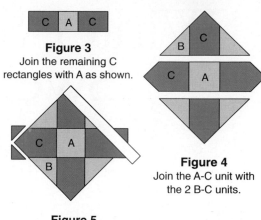

**Figure 4**
Join the A-C unit with the 2 B-C units.

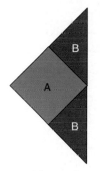

**Figure 5**
Trim excess C.

**Step 9.** Sew a D triangle to each burgundy plaid B side of the pieced unit to complete the pieced top referring to Figure 7; press seams toward D.

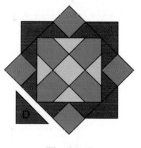

**Figure 6**
Sew a burgundy plaid B triangle to adjacent sides of a green floral A square.

**Figure 7**
Sew a D triangle to each burgundy plaid B side of the pieced unit to complete the pieced top.

**Step 10.** Lay batting on a flat surface; place prepared backing piece on batting right side up. Place the pieced top right sides together with backing piece. Pin to keep layers flat.

**Step 11.** Stitch all around edges using a 1/4" seam allowance, leaving an 8" opening on one side.

**Step 12.** Trim batting and backing even with quilt top edge; clip corners and points. Turn quilt right side out through opening.

**Step 13.** Hand-stitch opening closed. Quilt as desired by hand or machine. *Note: Sample shown was hand-quilted 1/4" from all seams using thread to match fabrics.*

**Step 14.** Sew one or two tassels at each corner, alternating colors referring to the photo and the Placement Diagram. ❧

# Winter Snowflake Sweatshirt

By Marian Shenk

*Dress up a sweatshirt with a simple snowflake design using our pattern.*
*If you like the technique, design one of your own.*

### Project Specifications

**Skill Level:** Beginner
**Project Size:** Size Varies

### Materials

- 1 adult-size deep blue sweatshirt
- 1/3 yard medium blue print
- 3 (5" x 5") squares navy blue solid
- Navy blue all-purpose thread
- Basic sewing supplies and tools

**Winter Snowflake Sweatshirt**
Placement Diagram
Size Varies

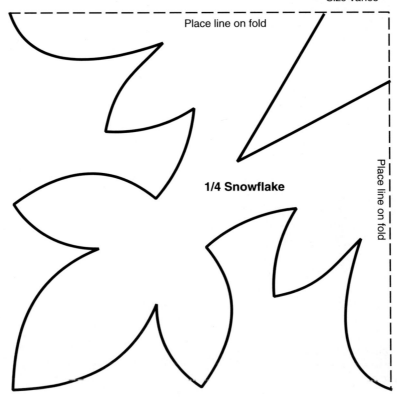

Place line on fold

**1/4 Snowflake**

Place line on fold

## Instructions

**Step 1.** Cut three 10" x 10" squares medium blue print. Fold each square in half and in half again to make a folded 5" x 5" square.

**Step 2.** Prepare a template using the 1/4 snowflake pattern given.

**Step 3.** Pin pattern piece on one folded square, matching edges of pattern with folds of square as shown in Figure 1. Cut out shape; repeat for three shapes.

**Figure 1**
Pin pattern piece on 1 folded square, matching edges of pattern with folds of square.

**Step 4.** Pin a 5" x 5" square navy blue solid under the center opening of each snowflake design. Trim the navy blue solid squares 1/4" beyond opening size.

**Step 5.** Arrange the three snowflake motifs on the sweatshirt front referring to the Placement Diagram and photo of project for positioning; pin and baste each motif to secure in place.

**Step 6.** Using a medium-width machine satin stitch, sew around centers and outside edges of each motif to finish. ❧

# Monarch Butterfly Pillow

By Connie Kauffman

*Combine a colorful butterfly print with this appliqué butterfly design to make a bright, summertime pillow.*

## Project Specifications

**Skill Level:** Beginner
**Project Size:** 16" x 16"

## Materials

- 1/4 yard light green batik
- 1/4 yard black solid
- 1/4 yard orange batik
- 1/2 yard green-and-yellow butterfly batik
- 1/2 yard white backing fabric
- 2 squares batting 16 1/2" x 16 1/2"
- 16" x 16" pillow form
- Green, black and orange all-purpose thread
- Orange-variegated rayon thread
- Black and green rayon thread
- 2 yards 8mm cord
- Fabric adhesive spray
- Basic sewing supplies and tools, zipper foot and newspaper

**Monarch Butterfly Pillow**
Placement Diagram
16" x 16"

## Instructions

**Step 1.** Cut one square green-and-yellow butterfly batik 16 1/2" x 16 1/2" for pillow back; repeat for two white backing fabric squares. Set aside.

**Step 2.** Cut one square light green batik 8 1/2" x 8 1/2" for center square. Cut two strips each green-and-yellow butterfly batik 4 1/2" x 8 1/2" and 4 1/2" x 16 1/2". Sew the shorter strips to two opposite sides of the center square and the longer strips to the remaining sides; press seams toward strips.

**Step 3.** Prepare pattern for butterfly shape referring to the General Instructions for machine appliqué.

**Step 4.** Cut shapes as directed on each piece. Lay the butterfly body face down on newspaper;

spray lightly with fabric adhesive spray referring to manufacturer's instructions.

**Step 5.** Position the body piece on the pieced section referring to the Placement Diagram and photo of project for positioning; press in place with your hand.

**Step 6.** Prepare inside body pieces and position on body as in Steps 3–5. **Note:** *It helps to spray the newspaper with adhesive spray before placing smaller pieces on top. The force of the spray is enough to blow smaller pieces away and the adhesive on the newspaper holds them in place. It will not adhere to the right side of the pieces even though they are touching the paper.*

**Step 7.** Using black rayon thread in the top of the machine and matching all-purpose thread in the bobbin, machine satin-stitch around the body

Figure 1. Trim seam to 1/4";
press seam open. Fold one end
over 1/4" press.

**Figure 1**
Join strips on short
ends as shown.

**Step 11.** Fold strip over cord to
prepare corded piping; using a
zipper foot, stitch close to cord .
as shown in Figure 2.

**Figure 2**
Stitch close to cord as shown.

**Step 12.** Cut two strips black
solid 1" x 34"; join strips on short
ends to make one long strip. Trim
seam to 1/4" and press open.
Fold strip in half along length
with wrong sides together; press.

**Step 13.** Lay the folded black
strip on top of piped cording
strip matching raw edges as
shown in Figure 3; machine
baste in place.

**Figure 3**
Lay the folded black strip on
top of piped cording strip
matching raw edges.

and straight-stitch antennae and lines on inside
body pieces referring to lines marked on pattern.
Repeat on inside pieces using orange-variegated
rayon thread in the top of the machine and
matching all-purpose thread in the bobbin.

**Step 8.** Spray the wrong side of the appliquéd
top and the white backing piece with fabric
adhesive spray; layer batting between pieces
with appliquéd top right side up. Repeat with
white backing and green-and-yellow butterfly
batik pillow back.

**Step 9.** Using green rayon thread in the top of
the machine and matching all-purpose thread in
the bobbin, machine-quilt diagonal lines on the
appliquéd center square background, around
butterfly shape and in the ditch between center
and borders. Quilt a meandering design on border strips. Repeat a meandering design on pillow back layers.

**Step 10.** Cut two strips orange batik 1 3/4" x
34"; join strips on short ends as shown in

**Step 14.** Using a small round lid or plate,
round the corners on quilted pillow top and
back as shown in Figure 4.

**Step 15.** Pin the unpressed end of the
piped cording to the edge of the pillow top with black strip touching
pillow top as shown in Figure 5;
continue pinning all around. At
end, insert beginning end
inside folded end as shown
in Figure 6. Machine-
baste to hold.

**Step 16.** Lay the quilted pillow back right

**Figure 4**
Using a small round lid or
plate, round the corners on
quilted pillow top and back.

**Figure 5**
Pin the unpressed end of the
piped cording to the edge of
the pillow top with black strip
touching pillow top.

**Figure 6**
Insert beginning end inside
folded end as shown.

sides together with pillow front; pin. Sew
together just outside of previously stitched basting line, leaving a 6" opening on one side; trim
seams when stitching is complete. Turn right
side out through opening.

**Step 17.** Insert pillow form; hand-stitch opening closed to finish. ❧

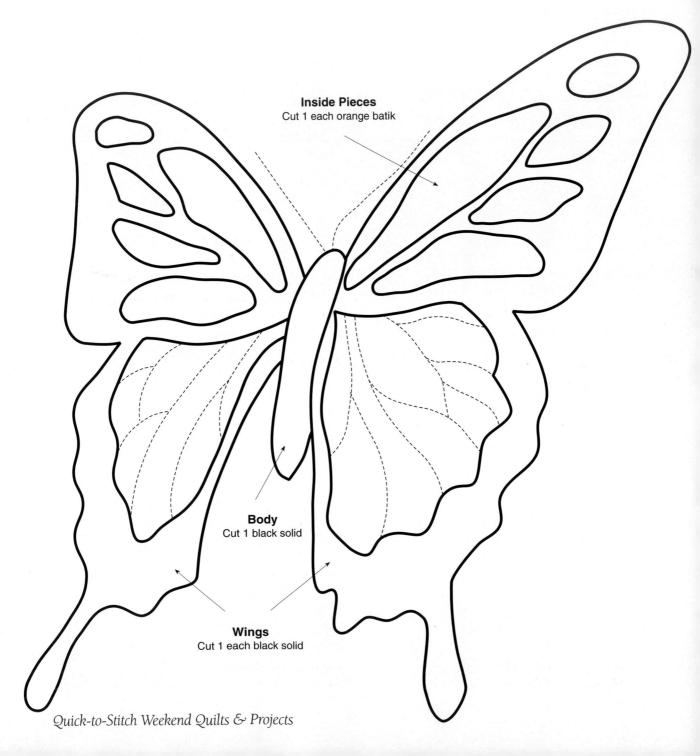

**Inside Pieces**
Cut 1 each orange batik

**Body**
Cut 1 black solid

**Wings**
Cut 1 each black solid

# Spring Flowers Coaster Set

By Kate Laucomer

*Bring spring flowers inside with this foundation-pieced coaster set made in seasonal colors.*

## Project Specifications

**Skill Level:** Intermediate
**Project Size:** 5 1/2" x 5 1/2" (includes binding)

## Materials

- Scraps green, pink, yellow and purple prints
- 3/8 yard white-on-white print
- 3/8 yard green print
- 4 squares batting 6" x 6"
- All-purpose thread to match fabrics
- Basic sewing supplies and tools and tracing paper

## Instructions

**Step 1.** Transfer each flower design to tracing paper using full-size patterns given; patterns are already reversed.

**Step 2.** Choose one design to begin and cut a piece to cover area 1 with excess being at least 1/4" larger all around; repeat for all pieces, referring to patterns for piece numbers and color.

**Step 3.** Lay piece #1 on unmarked side of tracing paper pattern referring to lines as they show through as shown in Figure 1. **Note:** *Refer to the General Instructions and page 17 for more details about foundation piecing.*

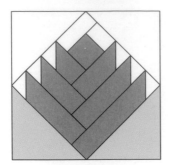

**Hyacinth Coaster**
Placement Diagram
5 1/2" x 5 1/2"
(includes binding)

**Step 4.** Pin piece #2 on piece #1; turn paper over and stitch on marked line as shown in Figure 2.

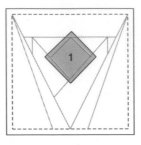

**Figure 1**
Lay piece #1 on unmarked side of tracing paper pattern referring to lines as they show through as shown.

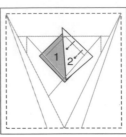
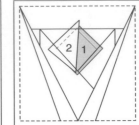

**Figure 2**
Pin piece #2 on piece #1; turn paper over and stitch on marked line as shown.

**Step 5.** Turn paper over again; trim excess to 1/8"–1/4" seam allowance. Press piece #2 flat as shown in Figure 3.

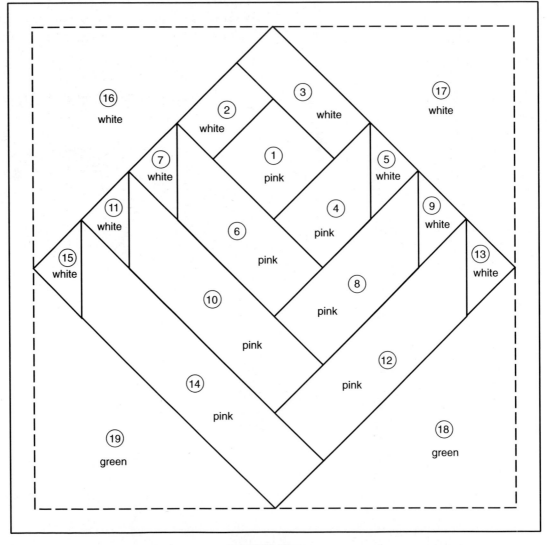

**Hyacinth Pattern**
Trace the full-size pattern onto tracing paper; pattern is already reversed.

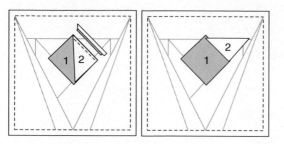

**Figure 3**
Trim excess to 1/8"–1/4" seam allowance.
Press piece #2 flat as shown.

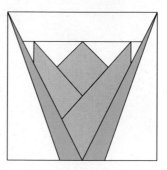

**Crocus Coaster**
Placement Diagram
5 1/2" x 5 1/2"
(includes binding)

**Step 6.** Continue adding pieces in numerical order until entire paper is covered.

**Step 7.** Trim excess to paper edge, which includes a 1/4" seam allowance; remove paper. Repeat for each design.

**Step 8.** Cut four 6" x 6" backing squares green print.

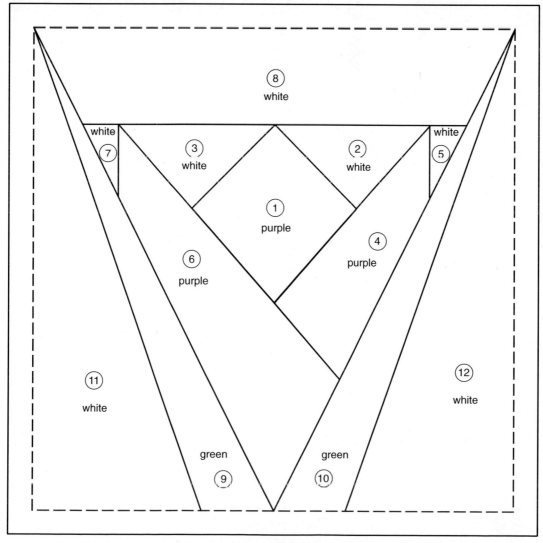

**Crocus Pattern**
Trace the full-size pattern onto tracing paper; pattern is already reversed.

**Tulip 2 Coaster**
Placement Diagram
5 1/2" x 5 1/2"
(includes binding)

Sandwich one batting square between one pieced top and one backing square; pin or baste layers together.

**Step 9.** Outline-quilt flower shape using all-purpose thread to match fabrics. When quilting is complete, trim edges even; remove pins or basting.

**Step 10.** Repeat for each flower shape.

**Step 11.** Cut three 2" by fabric width strips green print. Join strips on short ends to make one long strip. Bind edges of each coaster referring to the General Instructions to finish. ❧

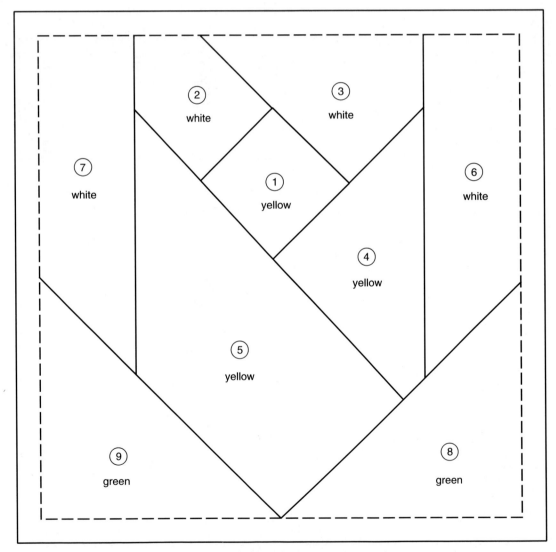

**Tulip 2 Pattern**
Trace the full-size pattern onto tracing paper; pattern is already reversed.

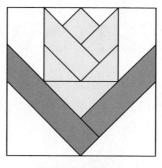

**Tulip 1 Coaster**
Placement Diagram
5 1/2" x 5 1/2"
(includes binding)

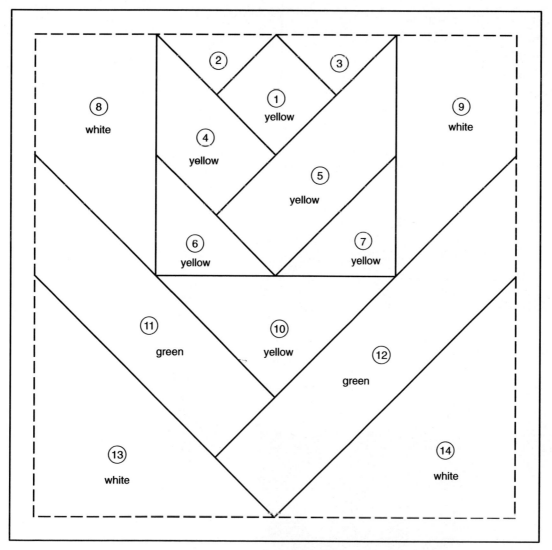

**Tulip 1 Pattern**
Trace the full-size pattern onto tracing paper; pattern is already reversed.

# Baby Bear Sweatshirt

By Marian Shenk

*Teddy bears are a child's best friend. Decorate the front of a plain sweatshirt with this teddy bear motif and their friend can be with them no matter where they go.*

## Project Specifications

**Skill Level:** Beginner
**Project Size:** Size Varies

## Materials

- 1 child-size blue sweatshirt
- Scraps brown velour
- Scraps brown solid and red print
- Brown all-purpose thread
- 1/4 yard 3/8"-wide blue satin ribbon
- 1/4 yard fusible transfer web
- Black and brown permanent fabric pens
- Basic sewing supplies and tools

## Instructions

**Step 1.** Prepare templates for each appliqué shape using full-size pattern given.

**Step 2.** Trace each shape on the paper side of the fusible transfer web referring to the General Instructions.

**Step 3.** Cut out shapes, leaving a margin around each one. Fuse paper shapes to the wrong side of the fabrics as directed on each piece for color; cut out on traced lines. Remove paper backing.

**Step 4.** Center and position fused shapes on the sweatshirt referring to pattern for order of placement; fuse shapes in place.

**Step 5.** Machine-appliqué all bear body parts except muzzle in place using a medium-width satin stitch.

**Step 6.** Outline shirt pieces using black permanent fabric pen as shown in Figure 1 (page 38). Outline muzzle using brown permanent fabric pen. Add muzzle details and eyes using black permanent pen and referring to pattern for positioning.

**Step 7.** Tie a bow with the blue satin ribbon. Hand-stitch the bow in place where indicated with an X on the pattern to finish. ❧

**Baby Bear Sweatshirt**
Placement Diagram
Size Varies

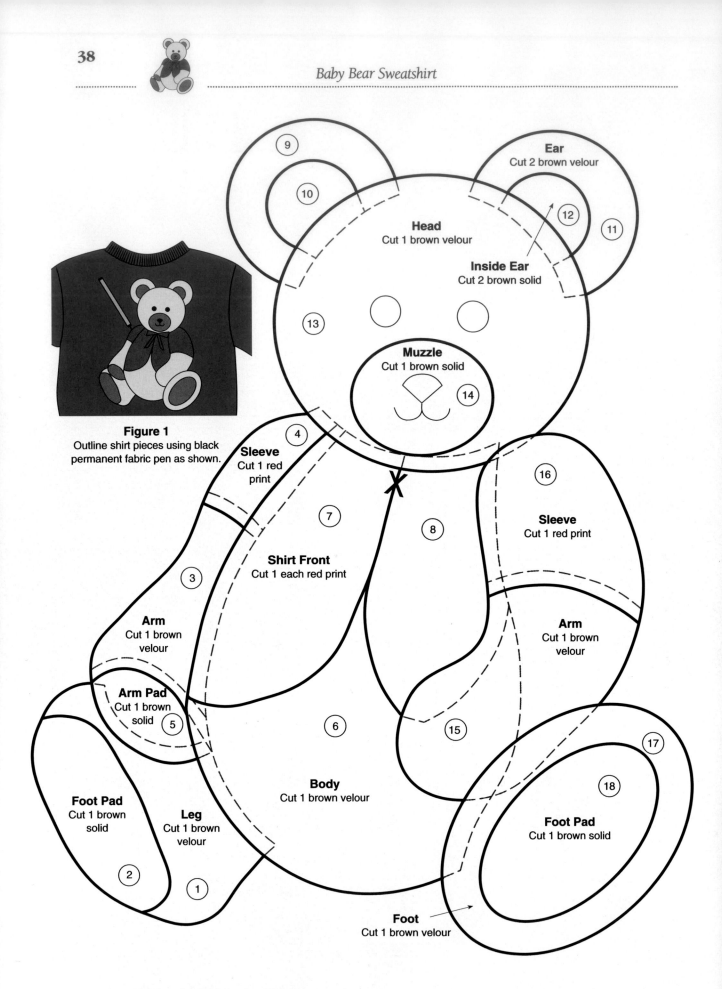

**Ear**
Cut 2 brown velour

**Head**
Cut 1 brown velour

**Inside Ear**
Cut 2 brown solid

**Muzzle**
Cut 1 brown solid

**Figure 1**
Outline shirt pieces using black
permanent fabric pen as shown.

**Sleeve**
Cut 1 red
print

**Sleeve**
Cut 1 red print

**Shirt Front**
Cut 1 each red print

**Arm**
Cut 1 brown
velour

**Arm**
Cut 1 brown
velour

**Arm Pad**
Cut 1 brown
solid

**Foot Pad**
Cut 1 brown
solid

**Leg**
Cut 1 brown
velour

**Body**
Cut 1 brown velour

**Foot Pad**
Cut 1 brown solid

**Foot**
Cut 1 brown velour

# Bear & 'Coon Bibs

By Kathy Brown

*Baby bibs with faces are simple and fun to make.*
*These bear and raccoon faces are sure to entertain Baby.*

## Bobbi Bear

### Project Specifications

**Skill Level:** Beginner
**Project Size:** 9" x 12"

### Materials

- 1/2 yard brown print
- Scraps black solid and tan and pink prints
- Batting 16" x 16"
- All-purpose thread to match fabrics
- Black all-purpose thread
- 1/4 yard fusible transfer web
- 2 (7/16") black ball buttons
- 1" square hook-and-loop tape
- Basic sewing supplies and tools

## Instructions

**Step 1.** Prepare template for bib piece; cut as directed on piece for Bobbi Bear. Repeat with ear piece.

**Step 2.** Prepare patterns for Bobbi Bear appliqué shapes using patterns given. Trace shapes on the paper side of the fusible transfer web as directed on shapes for number to cut. Cut out shapes, leaving a margin around each one.

**Step 3.** Fuse shapes to the wrong side of fabrics as indicated on pattern for color to cut; cut out shapes on traced lines. Remove paper backing.

**Step 4.** Arrange and fuse shapes to one brown print bib piece referring to pattern for order of

placement; fuse in place. Pin batting piece to the wrong side of the fused front.

**Step 5.** Using all-purpose thread to match fabrics and a medium-width machine zigzag stitch, stitch around each shape, again in numerical order. Transfer mouth lines to muzzle; stitch using black all-purpose thread and a medium-width zigzag stitch.

**Step 6.** Fuse inside ear pieces to a pair of ear pieces; pin batting to wrong side of fused ears. Appliqué inside ear pieces in place as in Step 5. Place one appliquéd and one plain ear piece right sides together; sew around outside curved edges. Clip curves; trim seams. Turn right side out and press; repeat for two ears. Turn seam inside on edges of each piece; hand-stitch opening closed. Set aside.

**Step 7.** Place appliquéd front right sides together with second bib piece; stitch around outside edges leaving an opening as marked on pattern. Clip seams and curves; turn right side out through opening. Press; hand-stitch opening closed.

**Step 8.** Pin assembled ear to bib front as indicated on pattern for placement; hand-stitch in place so ears stand up. ***Note:*** *Project has ears stitched on by machine with wide zigzag stitch.*

**Step 9.** Hand-sew buttons in place for eyes.

**Step 10.** Hand-stitch hook-and-loop tape to top edges on bib ends to finish.

## Richie Raccoon

| Project Specifications |
| --- |
| **Skill Level:** Beginner |
| **Project Size:** 9" x 12" |

| Materials |
| --- |
| • 1/2 yard brown print |
| • Scraps black solid and gray and pink prints |
| • Batting 16" x 16" |
| • All-purpose thread to match fabrics |
| • Black and gray all-purpose thread |
| • 1/4 yard fusible transfer web |
| • 2 (7/16") white ball buttons |
| • Black permanent marker to color button |
| • 1" square hook-and-loop tape |
| • Basic sewing supplies and tools |

### Instructions

**Step 1.** Prepare bib and appliqué pieces as for Bobbi Bear using Richie Raccoon pieces.

**Step 2.** Fuse and appliqué pieces in place and finish bib as for Bobbi Bear except add black dots to white ball buttons using black permanent marker. ❧

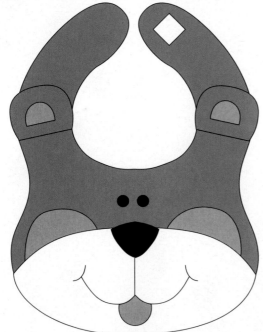

**Bobbi Bear**
Placement Diagram
9" x 12"

**Richie Raccoon**
Placement Diagram
9" x 12"

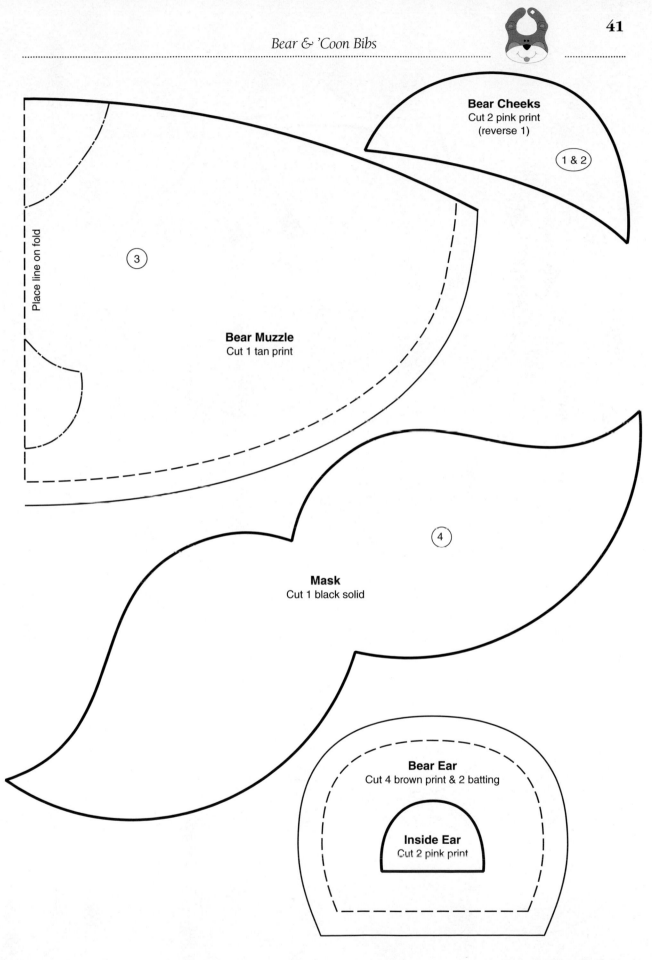

**Bear Cheeks**
Cut 2 pink print
(reverse 1)

1 & 2

3

Place line on fold

**Bear Muzzle**
Cut 1 tan print

4

**Mask**
Cut 1 black solid

**Bear Ear**
Cut 4 brown print & 2 batting

**Inside Ear**
Cut 2 pink print

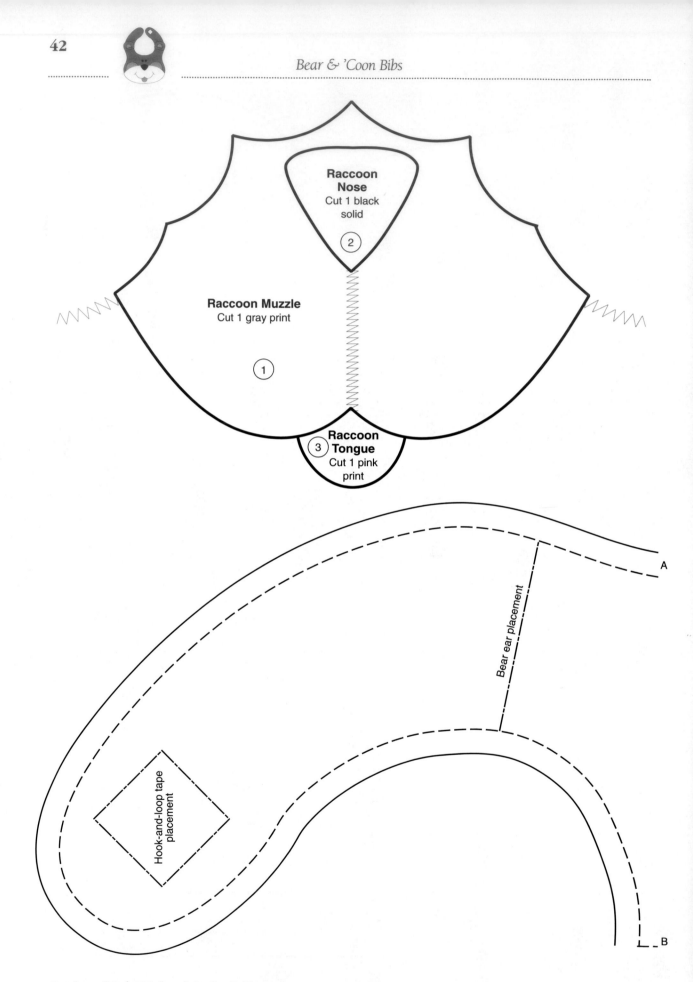

**Raccoon Nose**
Cut 1 black solid
②

**Raccoon Muzzle**
Cut 1 gray print
①

③ **Raccoon Tongue**
Cut 1 pink print

A

Bear ear placement

Hook-and-loop tape placement

B

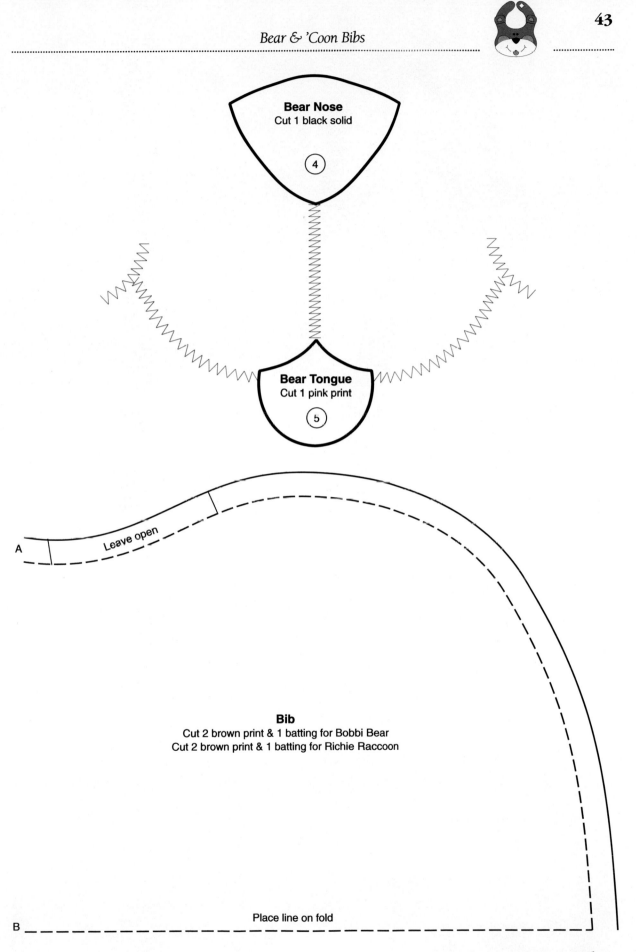

**Bear Nose**
Cut 1 black solid

④

**Bear Tongue**
Cut 1 pink print

⑤

A

Leave open

**Bib**
Cut 2 brown print & 1 batting for Bobbi Bear
Cut 2 brown print & 1 batting for Richie Raccoon

Place line on fold

B

# The Christmas Home

*Put some Christmas music on the stereo, round up your stash of fabrics and get in the holiday mood while stitching up a special quilted Christmas project.*

*In 20 hours or less you can complete one of the many wonderful projects included in this chapter. Whether you need a table runner, place mat, garment, tree skirt, mantel cover or more, there is something here for you.*

*Make one for yourself and one for a special gift while spreading the holiday spirit in your home and to your family.*

# Happy Holiday Mother/Daughter Cardigan

By Janice Loewenthal

*Dress for warmth during the holiday season with these embellished sweatshirts.*

## Mother's Cardigan

### Project Specifications

**Skill Level:** Intermediate
**Project Size:** Size varies
**Block Size:** 3" x 3"
**Number of Blocks:** 14 pieced; 14 appliquéd

### Materials

- 1 cream adult-size sweatshirt
- Scraps of white, gold, black and burgundy solids or prints for appliqué
- 1/4 yard each navy, blue and gold prints and burgundy solid
- 1/3 yard burgundy dot
- All-purpose thread to match appliqué fabrics
- 1/2 yard fusible transfer web
- 1/3 yard tear-off fabric stabilizer
- Black permanent fine-point pen
- White acrylic paint and paintbrush
- Make-up blusher
- Basic sewing supplies and tools, seam ripper, rotary cutter, mat and ruler

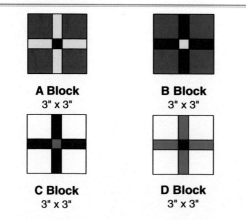

**A Block**
3" x 3"

**B Block**
3" x 3"

**C Block**
3" x 3"

**D Block**
3" x 3"

Because of size differences, we know that all sweatshirts will not use the same number of pieced and appliquéd blocks. The instructions are given to make the sweatshirt as shown; adjust the number of blocks needed for your size sweatshirt.

## Instructions

**Step 1.** Wash and dry sweatshirt; do not use fabric softener.

**Step 2.** Carefully remove bottom band from sweatshirt using a seam ripper. Smooth out shirt onto the cutting surface and cut with a rotary cutter to make a straight edge. Mark the center front of the shirt; cut to make opening. Stitch 1/8" from outer edge to prevent stretching.

**Step 3.** Measure the distance around the sweatshirt bottom and divide by 3 (size of finished blocks). Trim a small amount off each side of the front opening, if necessary to fit an even number of blocks. *Note: If the shirt measures 44", trim 3/4" off each front side to make 42 1/2" (includes seam allowance).*

**Step 4.** Cut two strips each navy and gold prints 1 3/4" by fabric width. Cut one strip each gold print and burgundy solid 1" by fabric width.

**Step 5.** Sew a 1" gold print strip between two 1 3/4" navy print strips along length with right sides together; press seams toward darker fabric. Subcut strip set into 1 3/4" segments as shown in Figure 1.

**Step 6.** Sew a 1" burgundy solid strip between two 1 3/4" gold print strips along length with right sides together; press seams toward darker

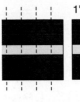

**Mother's Cardigan**
Placement Diagram
Size Varies

**Step 10.** Sew a 1" gold print strip between two 1 3/4" burgundy solid strips along length with right sides together; press seams toward darker fabric. Subcut strip set into 1" segments as shown in Figure 5.

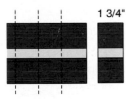

**Figure 5**
Subcut strip set into 1"
segments as shown.

fabric. Subcut strip set into 1" segments as shown in Figure 2.

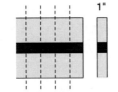

**Figure 1**
Subcut strip set into 1 3/4"
segments as shown.

**Figure 2**
Subcut strip set into 1"
segments as shown.

**Step 11.** Sew a burgundy/gold/burgundy segment between two navy/burgundy/navy segments to make one B block as shown in Figure 6; repeat for six B blocks.

**Figure 6**
Join segments to
make 1 B block.

**Step 12.** Cut 14 squares blue print 3 1/2" x 3 1/2".

**Step 13.** Prepare templates for snowman, mitten and heart appliqué shapes using patterns given. Trace shapes on the paper side of the fusible transfer web referring to pattern for number to cut. Cut out shapes leaving a margin around each one.

**Step 7.** Sew a gold/burgundy/gold segment between two navy/gold/navy segments to make one A block as shown in Figure 3; repeat for eight A blocks.

**Figure 3**
Join segments as shown
to make 1 A block.

**Step 8.** Cut two strips each navy print and burgundy solid 1 3/4" by fabric width. Cut one strip each gold print and burgundy solid 1" by fabric width.

**Step 9.** Sew a 1" burgundy solid strip between two 1 3/4" navy print strips along length with right sides together; press seams toward darker fabric. Subcut strip set into 1 3/4" segments as shown in Figure 4.

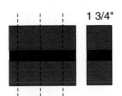

**Figure 4**
Subcut strip set into 1 3/4"
segments as shown.

**Step 14.** Fuse paper shapes to the wrong side of fabric scraps referring to pattern for color; cut out shapes on traced lines. Remove paper backing.

**Step 15.** Center and arrange shapes on the 3 1/2" x 3 1/2" blue print squares, referring to patterns for order of arrangement. ***Note:*** *Place two mittens on a square, one overlapping the other, as shown in the Placement Diagram.* Fuse shapes in place when satisfied with arrangement.

**Step 16.** Cut a square of tear-off fabric stabilizer for each appliquéd square; pin in place. Using thread to match fabrics, machine satin-stitch each snowman shape in place. Add nose detail to snowman using orange thread and hatband detail line using red thread.

**Step 17.** Using black all-purpose thread, machine buttonhole-stitch the mitten and heart pieces in place.

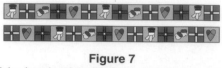

**Step 18.** Join pieced and appliquéd blocks as shown in Figure 7 to make a row; repeat for second row, again referring to Figure 7.

**Figure 7**
Join pieced and appliquéd blocks to make a row.

**Step 19.** Join the rows along length to make bottom panel.

**Step 20.** Cut two strips burgundy dot 1 3/4" by length of pieced panel; sew a strip to the top and bottom of the pieced panel. Press seams toward strips.

**Step 21.** Pin the right side of the pieced panel to the wrong side of the sweatshirt along the bottom edge; stitch along bottom edge using a 1/4" seam allowance.

**Step 22.** Press panel to front of shirt. Turn under remaining long edge of pieced panel 1/4"; pin panel in place on sweatshirt front. Topstitch 1/8" from each edge of bottom burgundy strip and 1/8" from each edge of top burgundy strip.

**Step 23.** Cut two strips 4 1/2" wide and 1/2" longer than the front edge measurement. Pin a strip to each front edge with right sides together; stitch. Press seams toward strips.

**Step 24.** Press over remaining raw edge of each strip 1/4". Turn ends of strips under even with edge of sweatshirt bottom and neckline; press to hold.

**Step 25.** Fold strip to the wrong side and over seam as shown in Figure 8; baste to hold in place. Topstitch along strip edges as shown in Figure 9 to finish.

**Figure 8**
Fold strip to the wrong side
and over seam as shown.

**Figure 9**
Topstitch along strip
edges as shown.

**Step 26.** Add two black dots to snowmen for eyes and draw mouth using black permanent fine-point pen. Add whites of eyes using white acrylic paint and paintbrush. Add checks using make-up blusher.

## Child's Cardigan

| Project Specifications |
| --- |
| **Skill Level:** Intermediate |
| **Project Size:** Size varies |
| **Block Size:** 3" x 3" |
| **Number of Blocks:** 5 pieced; 4 appliquéd |

| Materials |
| --- |
| • 1 cream child-size sweatshirt |
| • Scraps of tan, green, gold and burgundy solids or prints for appliqué |
| • 1 fat quarter each burgundy solid, cream print and green mottled |
| • 1/3 yard burgundy/green/cream check |
| • All-purpose thread to match appliqué fabrics |
| • 1/8 yard fusible transfer web |
| • 1/8 yard tear-off fabric stabilizer |
| • Black permanent fine-point pen |
| • White acrylic paint and paintbrush |
| • Make-up blusher |
| • Basic sewing supplies and tools, seam ripper, rotary cutter, mat and ruler |

This child's sweatshirt has only one row of blocks. It uses different colored fabrics than the adult-size sweatshirt but the blocks are pieced in the same manner.

**Child's Cardigan**
Placement Diagram
Size Varies

## Instructions

**Step 1.** Prepare sweatshirt as in Steps 1–3 for Mother's Cardigan.

**Step 2.** Cut two strips each cream print and burgundy solid 1 3/4" x 22". Cut one strip each burgundy solid and green mottled 1" x 22".

**Step 3.** Sew a 1" burgundy solid strip between two 1 3/4" cream print strips along length with right sides together; press seams toward darker fabric. Subcut strip set into 1 3/4" segments as shown in Figure 10.

**Step 4.** Sew a 1" green mottled strip between two 1 3/4" burgundy solid strips along length with right sides together; press seams toward darker fabric. Subcut strip set into 1" segments as shown in Figure 11.

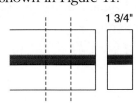

**Figure 10**
Subcut strip set into 1 3/4" segments.

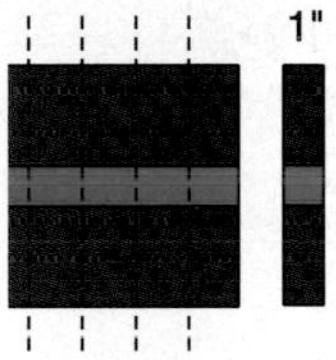

**Figure 11**
Subcut strip set into 1" segments.

**Step 5.** Sew a burgundy/green/burgundy segment between two cream/burgundy/cream segments to make one C block as shown in Figure 12; repeat for three C blocks.

**Step 6.** Cut two strips each cream print and green mottled 1 3/4" x 22". Cut one strip each burgundy solid and green mottled 1" x 22".

**Step 7.** Sew a 1" green mottled strip between two 1 3/4" cream print strips along length with right sides together; press seams toward darker fabric. Subcut strip set into 1 3/4" segments as shown in Figure 13.

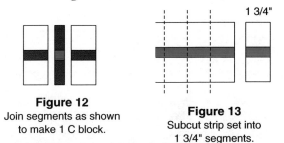

**Figure 12**
Join segments as shown to make 1 C block.

**Figure 13**
Subcut strip set into 1 3/4" segments.

**Step 8.** Sew a 1" burgundy solid strip between two 1 3/4" green mottled strips along length with right sides together; press seams toward darker fabric. Subcut strip set into 1" segments as shown in Figure 14.

**Step 9.** Sew a green/burgundy/green segment between two cream/green/cream segments to make one D block as shown in Figure 15; repeat for two D blocks.

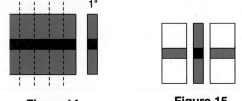

**Figure 14**
Subcut strip set into 1" segments.

**Figure 15**
Join segments as shown to make 1 D block.

**Step 10.** Cut two squares each burgundy solid and green mottled 3 1/2" x 3 1/2".

**Step 11.** Prepare tree, star and gingerbread man appliqué pieces and appliqué to squares referring to Steps 13–18 for Mother's Cardigan and to Figure 16 for joining squares to make pieced strip. *Note: Machine satin-stitch all appliqué shapes.*

**Figure 16**
Join pieced and appliquéd squares to make a strip.

**Step 12.** Cut two burgundy/green/cream check strips; apply to pieced strip and stitch strip to sweatshirt front as in Steps 20–22 for Mother's Cardigan except eliminate topstitching and use black all-purpose thread to machine buttonhole-stitch along edges of check strips.

**Step 13.** Cut two burgundy/green/cream check strips for front edges and apply as in Steps 23–25 for Mother's Cardigan.

**Step 14.** Add eyes and cheeks to gingerbread men as in Step 26 for Mother's Cardigan. Draw on mouth and nose using black permanent fine-point pen to finish. ❧

*Happy Holiday Mother/Daughter Cardigan appliqué pieces continued on page 52*

# Sing a Song of Christmas

By Holly Daniels

*Christmas prints and colors combine with strip piecing and
quick-sewing techniques to make this simple star-design quilt.*

## Project Specifications

**Skill Level:** Beginner
**Project Size:** 59" x 59"
**Blocks Size:** 15" x 15"
**Number of Block:** 9

## Materials

- 1 yard white solid
- 1/2 yard green print
- 1 1/8 yards red print
- 1 5/8 yards musical print
- Backing 63" x 63"
- Batting 63" x 63"
- 7 yards self-made or purchased binding
- White and green all-purpose thread
- Basic sewing supplies and tools

## Instructions

**Step 1.** Cut the following 3 3/8" by fabric width strips: five green print, nine each white solid and red print and two musical print.

**Step 2.** Cut each strip into 3 3/8" segments for A. You will need 16 musical print, 54 green print, 106 white solid and 108 red print A segments.

**Step 3.** Cut 20 red print squares in half on one diagonal to make 40 B triangles.

**Step 4.** Draw a diagonal line on the wrong side of each white solid, musical print and 18 green print A squares.

**Step 5.** Place a green print A right sides together with a red print A. Stitch 1/4" on each side of the drawn line as shown in Figure 1; cut apart on line to make two red/green A units. Repeat with all squares to make 36 red/green, 16 musical/white, 16 red/musical, 72 green/white and 124 red/white A units.

**Figure 1**
Stitch 1/4" on each
side of drawn line.

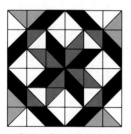

**Ohio Star Center**
15" x 15" Block
Make 1

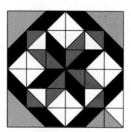

**Ohio Star Corner**
15" x 15" Block
Make 4

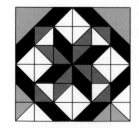

**Ohio Star Side**
15" x 15" Block
Make 4

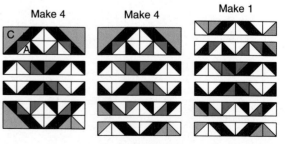

**Figure 2**
Arrange A units with B and C triangles to form blocks as shown.

**Step 6.** Cut two strips musical print 5 7/8" by fabric width; sub-cut into 5 7/8" squares. Cut each square on one diagonal to make 20 C triangles.

**Step 7.** Arrange A units with B and C triangles to form blocks referring to Figure 2. Join the units and triangles in rows; join rows to complete blocks.

**Step 8.** Arrange blocks in three rows of three blocks each, placing the Ohio Star Center block in the center and the Ohio Star Corner blocks in the corners referring to the Placement Diagram. Join blocks in rows; join rows to complete the pieced center.

**Step 9.** Cut and piece two strips each 3 1/2" x 45 1/2" and 3 1/2" x 51 1/2" musical print. Sew the shorter strips to opposite sides and longer strips to the top and

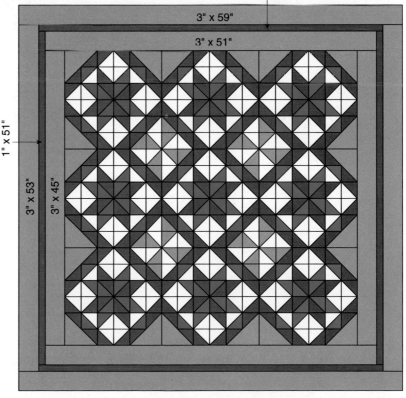

**Sing a Song of Christmas**
Placement Diagram
59" x 59"

bottom of the pieced center; press seams toward strips.

**Step 10.** Cut and piece two strips each 1 1/2" x 51 1/2" and 1 1/2" x 53 1/2" red print. Sew the shorter strips to opposite sides and longer strips to the top and bottom of the pieced center; press seams toward strips.

**Step 11.** Cut and piece two strips each 3 1/2" x 53 1/2" and 3 1/2" x 59 1/2" musical print. Sew

the shorter strips to opposite sides and longer strips to the top and bottom of the pieced center; press seams toward strips.

**Step 12.** Prepare quilt for quilting, quilt and bind with self-made or purchased binding referring to the General Instructions. ***Note:*** *The quilt shown was machine quilted in a meandering design using white all-purpose thread in the white areas and green all-purpose thread in the green pieces and borders.* ❧

*Happy Holiday Mother/Daughter Cardigan*
*Continued from page 49*

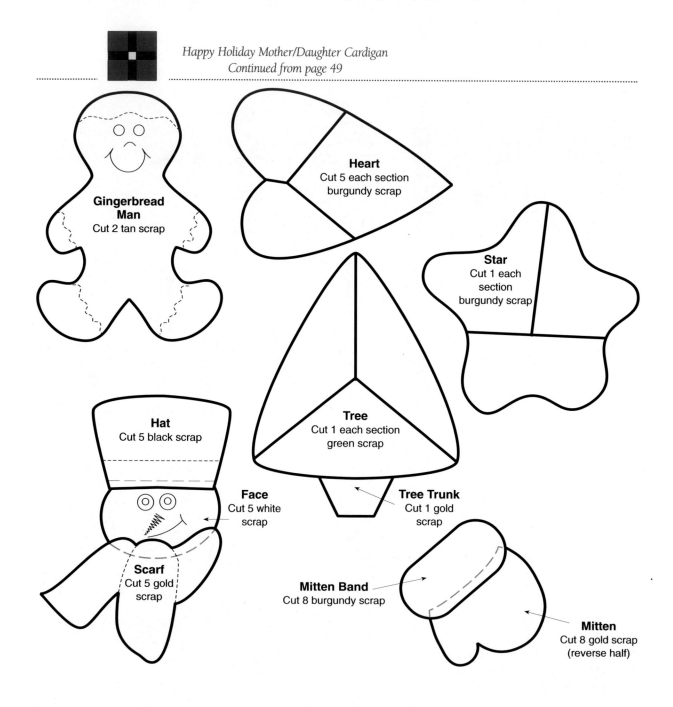

**Gingerbread Man**
Cut 2 tan scrap

**Heart**
Cut 5 each section
burgundy scrap

**Star**
Cut 1 each
section
burgundy scrap

**Tree**
Cut 1 each section
green scrap

**Hat**
Cut 5 black scrap

**Face**
Cut 5 white
scrap

**Scarf**
Cut 5 gold
scrap

**Tree Trunk**
Cut 1 gold
scrap

**Mitten Band**
Cut 8 burgundy scrap

**Mitten**
Cut 8 gold scrap
(reverse half)

# Wintry Log Cabin Lattice

By Pat Campbell

*The Log Cabin block has been used as the basis for beautiful quilted projects for over a hundred years and it is still a favorite among quilters as is evidenced by this holiday table runner.*

## Project Specifications

**Skill Level:** Intermediate

**Project Size:** 14 1/4" x 42 3/4"

**Block Size:** 5" x 5" and 5" x 5" x 7 1/8"

**Number of Blocks:** 16 and 8

## Materials

- 1/4 yard red print
- 3/8 yard green print
- 1/2 yard navy print
- 1/2 yard white print
- Backing 18" x 47"
- Neutral color all-purpose thread
- 1 1/4 yards lightweight fusible interfacing
- Basic sewing supplies and tools and press cloth

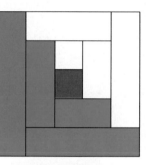

**Log Cabin**
5" x 5" Block

**Half Log Cabin**
5" x 5" x 7 1/8" Block

## Instructions

**Step 1.** Cut 2" by fabric width strips of the following: six strips navy print; four strips green print; two strips red print; and seven strips white print.

**Step 2.** Copy paper-piecing foundation patterns for the Log Cabin and Half Log Cabin blocks

referring to the patterns for number to copy.

**Step 3.** Referring to the General Instructions and page 17 for foundation-piecing instructions and using 2"-wide strips cut in Step 1, construct blocks starting with piece 1 and working in numerical order.

**Step 4.** Join four Log Cabin blocks as shown in Figure 1; repeat for three units.

**Step 5.** Join one Log Cabin block with two Half Log Cabin blocks as shown in Figure 2; repeat for four units.

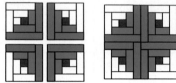

**Figure 1**
Join 4 Log Cabin blocks as shown.

**Figure 2**
Join 1 Log Cabin block with 2
Half Log Cabin blocks as shown.

**Step 6.** Join the units as shown in Figure 3 to complete pieced top; press seams open.

**Step 7.** Cut the lightweight fusible interfacing about 1/2" to 1" larger than the pieced top.

**Step 8.** Place a press cloth over the ironing board to prevent interfacing from sticking to your work area.

**Wintry Log Cabin Lattice**
Placement Diagram
14 1/4" x 42 3/4"

**Step 9.** Lay the interfacing (shiny side up) on the ironing board; position the pieced top wrong side on the interfacing with an even amount of excess interfacing showing all around. Press from the center to the outside but not closer than 1/2" from edges using a lift, move and press movement.

**Step 10.** Trim away excess interfacing; place press cloth over top and press edges to secure.

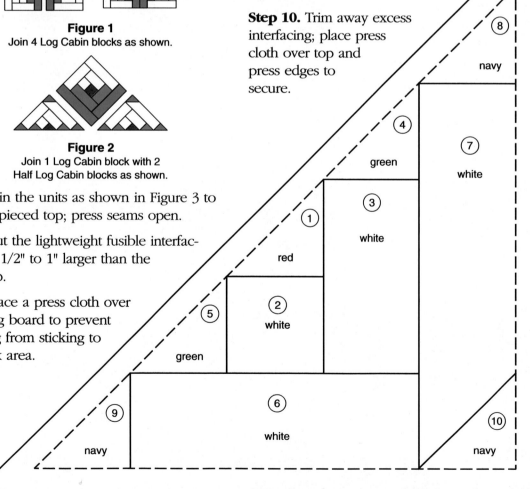

**Half Log Cabin Block**
Make 8

**Figure 3**
Join the units as shown to complete pieced top.

**Step 11.** Place the prepared backing and top

right sides together; pin. Trim backing even with top.

**Step 12.** Sew all around leaving a 5"–6" opening on one long side; clip corners and points. Turn right side out, pushing out corners with a blunt object. Flatten seams on edges and finger-press. Press with medium-hot steam iron.

**Step 13.** Turn raw seam edges to the inside at opening; hand-stitch opening closed to finish. ❧

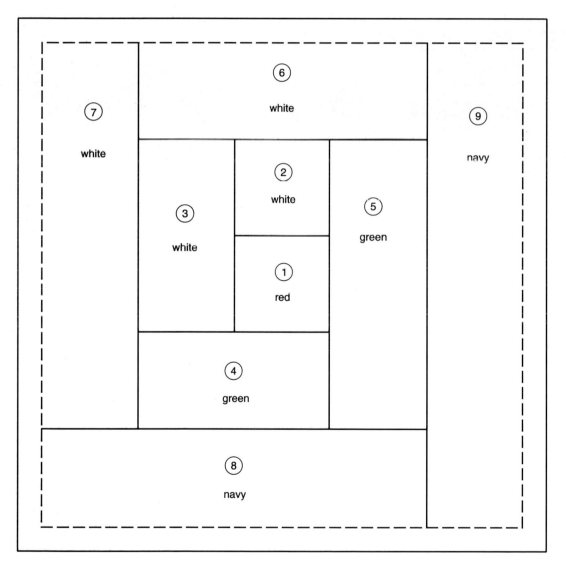

**Log Cabin Block**
Make 16

# Happy Holly Table Topper

By Kate Laucomer

*One simple holly leaf creates the wreath design on this pretty table topper.
Red buttons make the berries joining the leaves to create a three-dimensional look.
Crosshatch hand quilting adds an heirloom quality to a simple project.*

## Project Specifications

**Skill Level:** Beginner
**Project Size:** 24" x 24" (includes binding)

## Materials

- 24" x 24" square cream-on-cream print
- Assorted green print scraps
- Backing 28" x 28"
- Batting 28" x 28"
- 3 yards self-made or purchased binding
- Red and green all-purpose thread
- Cream hand-quilting thread
- 24 (3/8") red buttons
- 1/2 yard fusible transfer web
- 2/3 yard tear-off fabric stabilizer
- Black marker
- Basic sewing supplies and tools and large sheet of paper

**Happy Holly Table Topper**
Placement Diagram
24" x 24"
(includes binding)

## Instructions

**Step 1.** Draw a 16" circle on a large sheet of paper using a compass or large skillet lid. Trace over circle with a black marker.

**Step 2.** Trace 36 holly leaves on the paper side of the fusible transfer web. Cut out each shape, leaving a margin around each one. Fuse shapes to the wrong side of the green print scraps.

**Step 3.** Cut out shapes on traced lines; remove paper backing.

**Step 4.** Place marked paper under the cream-on-cream print background square; pin.

**Step 5.** Arrange holly leaves on the background square using marked line on paper as a guide to make the circle shape. **Note:** *Refer to the Placement Diagram for positioning and grouping suggestions. The project shown has three holly leaves in each corner and six in the centers of each side.* When satisfied with your arrangement, fuse shapes in place; remove paper from beneath the background.

**Step 6.** Place tear-off fabric stabilizer under fused shapes and using green all-purpose thread, machine satin-stitch around each leaf shape; tear off fabric stabilizer.

**Step 7.** Prepare quilt for quilting, quilt and finish with self-made or purchased binding referring to the General Instructions. **Note:** *The quilt*

shown was hand-quilted in a 3/4"
crosshatch quilting design using cream
quilting thread.

**Step 8.** Use all-purpose red thread to
sew three red buttons between corner
leaf groupings and side leaf groupings
referring to the photo of the project
and Placement Diagram for positioning
suggestions. ❧

**Holly Leaf**
Cut 36 green print scraps

*The Christmas Home*

# Patchwork Pine Trees & Stars

By Kate Laucomer

*Use Christmas fabrics or other seasonal prints to create*
*this table runner with appliquéd trees and stars.*

## Project Specifications

**Skill Level:** Beginner
**Project Size:** 16 1/2" x 40 1/2"

## Materials

- 12 squares various tan prints 6 1/2" x 6 1/2"
- Scraps green, tan and gold prints or plaids
- 1/8 yard green plaid
- 3/8 yard red plaid
- Backing 20" x 44"
- Batting 20" x 44"
- All-purpose thread to match fabrics
- Cream quilting thread
- Black 6-strand embroidery floss
- 1/2 yard fusible transfer web
- Basic sewing supplies and tools

## Instructions

**Step 1.** Trace six star and six tree shapes on the paper side of the fusible transfer web; cut out shapes, leaving a margin around each one.

**Step 2.** Fuse cut shapes to the wrong side of the green, tan and gold print or plaid scraps. Cut out shapes on traced lines; remove paper backing.

**Step 3.** Center and fuse a shape on each of the twelve 6 1/2" x 6 1/2" tan print squares.

**Step 4.** Using 2 strands black embroidery floss, blanket-stitch around each fused shape referring to the General Instructions.

**Step 5.** Arrange the appliquéd squares in two rows of six squares each referring to the Placement Diagram for positioning of squares. Join squares in rows; join rows. Press seams in one direction.

**Step 6.** Cut two strips each green plaid 1" x 13 1/2" and 1" x 36 1/2". Sew the longer strips to opposite long sides and shorter strips to each end; press seams toward strips.

**Step 7.** Cut two strips each red plaid 2 1/4" x 17" and 2 1/4" x 37 1/2". Sew the longer strips to opposite long sides and shorter strips to each end; press seams toward strips.

**Step 8.** Prepare for quilting and quilt referring to the General Instructions. ***Note:*** *The sample shown was hand-quilted around the appliqué shapes using cream quilting thread and machine-quilted in the ditch of the squares and border seams using all-purpose thread to match fabrics.*

**Step 9.** Prepare 3 1/2 yards self-made red plaid bias binding and finish edges referring to the General Instructions. ❧

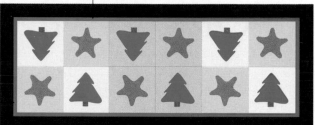

1/2" x 36"

1/2" x 13"

**Patchwork Pine Trees & Stars**
Placement Diagram
16 1/2" x 40 1/2"

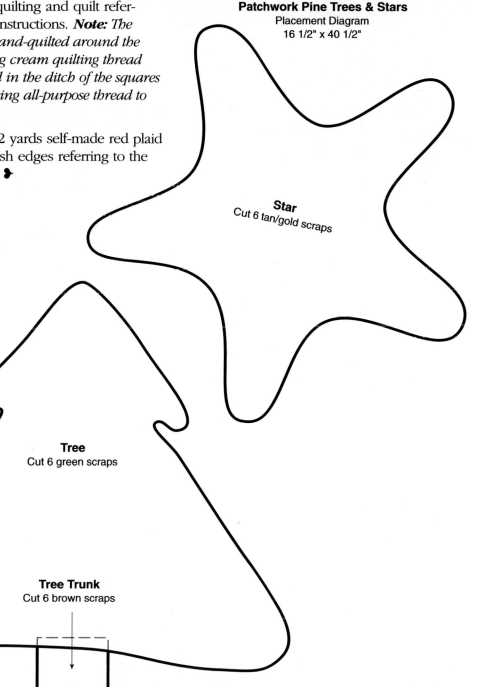

**Star**
Cut 6 tan/gold scraps

**Tree**
Cut 6 green scraps

**Tree Trunk**
Cut 6 brown scraps

# Jolly Santa Tree Skirt

By Janice Loewenthal

*Santa would be very pleased to place gifts under a tree
ringed with this happy-faced Santa tree skirt.*

## Project Specifications

**Skill Level:** Intermediate
**Project Size:** 49" diameter

## Materials

- Scraps pink and red flannel
- Scrap black solid
- 1/2 yard cream mottled
- 1 1/2 yards white flannel
- 2 1/4 yards red quilted flannel
- White, black, pink and red all-purpose thread
- 3 3/4 yards fusible transfer web
- Ecru 6-strand embroidery floss
- Basic sewing supplies and tools

**Jolly Santa Tree Skirt**
Placement Diagram
49" Diameter

Using purchased quilted flannel for the wedge shapes in this tree skirt eliminates the need for batting and backing fabrics. If you do not use quilted fabric, you will need to purchase backing and batting and the finished project will require quilting to hold the layers together. Purchased quilted fabric is recommended to complete this project in the least amount of time.

## Instructions

**Step 1.** Prepare template for wedge piece using pattern given and referring to Figure 1. Cut as directed on the pattern piece.

**Step 2.** Trace Santa appliqué shapes onto the paper side of the fusible transfer web referring to the patterns for number

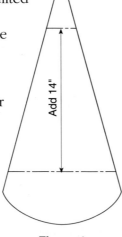

**Figure 1**
Prepare wedge
template as shown.

to cut. Cut out shapes, leaving a margin around each shape; fuse shapes to the wrong side of fabrics as directed on patterns for color. Cut out shapes on traced lines; remove paper backing.

**Step 3.** Position appliqué shapes on one wedge shape in numerical order, referring to the pattern and placing hatband 12 1/2" from point of wedge as shown in Figure 2. **Note:** *Be sure beard section is lined up with bottom edge of wedge shape.* Fuse shapes in place. Repeat for all 12 wedge shapes.

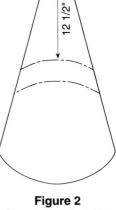

**Figure 2**
Place hatband 12 1/2"
from point of wedge.

**Step 4.** Machine satin-stitch around each shape using all-purpose thread for appliqué as follows: white for all white flannel pieces and bottom edge of mustache, red for lips, pink for nose and black for eyes.

**Step 5.** Using 2 strands ecru embroidery floss, stitch star shapes in the center of each eye using pattern given.

**Step 6.** Stitch the 12 wedge shapes together to make a circular shape, leaving one seam open.

**Step 7.** Lay stitched tree skirt on a flat surface. Using the A shape, cut center circle.

**Step 8.** Prepare 6 1/2 yards self-made white flannel bias binding and apply to all edges referring to the General Instructions. ❧

*The Christmas Home*

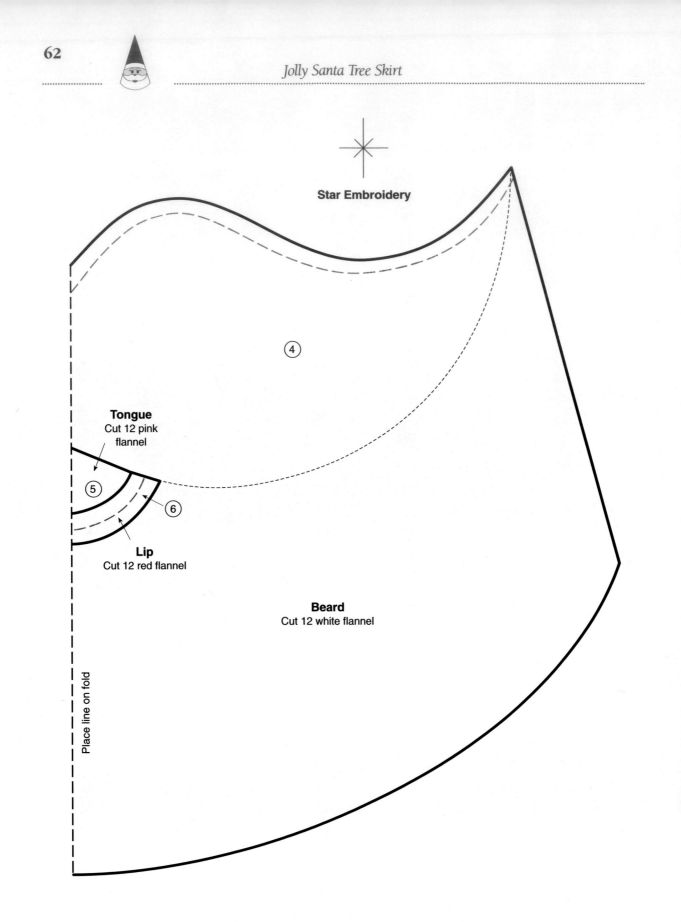

Star Embroidery

④

**Tongue**
Cut 12 pink
flannel

⑤

⑥

**Lip**
Cut 12 red flannel

**Beard**
Cut 12 white flannel

Place line on fold

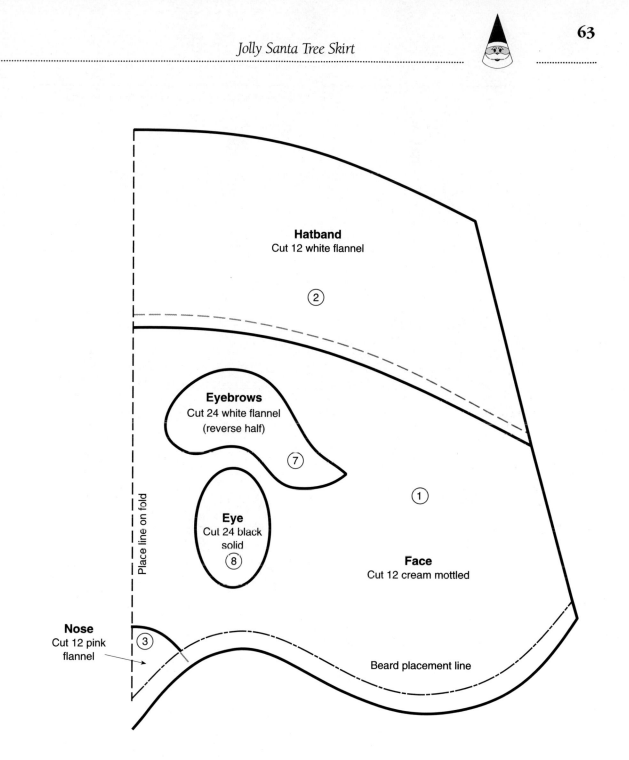

**Hatband**
Cut 12 white flannel

②

**Eyebrows**
Cut 24 white flannel
(reverse half)

⑦

①

**Eye**
Cut 24 black
solid

⑧

Place line on fold

**Face**
Cut 12 cream mottled

**Nose**
Cut 12 pink
flannel

③

Beard placement line

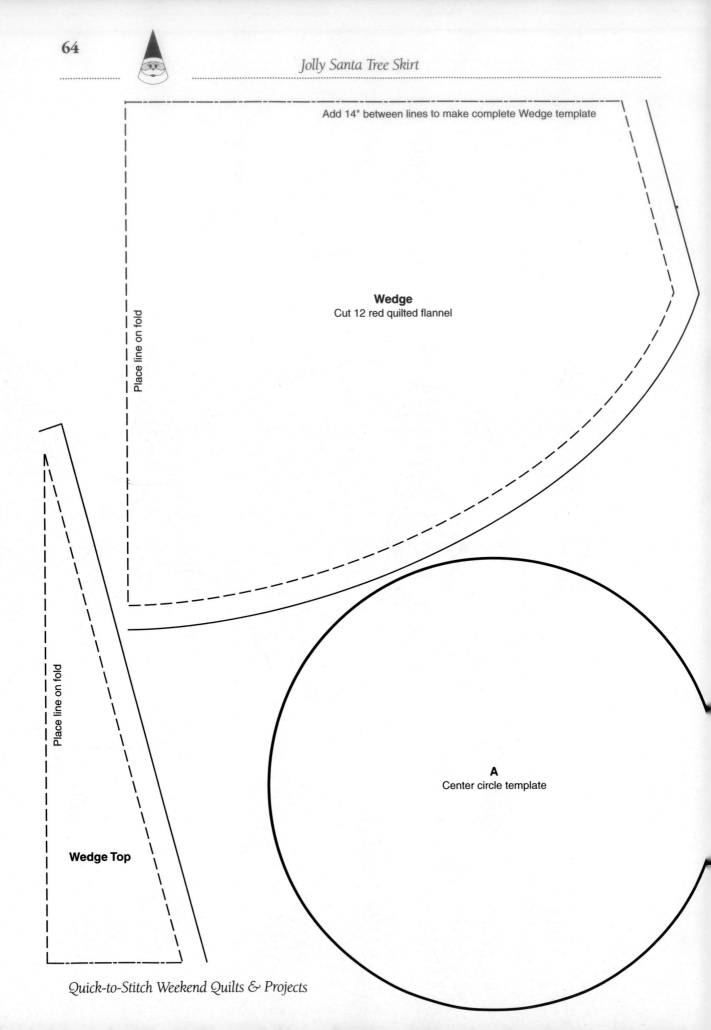

Add 14" between lines to make complete Wedge template

**Wedge**
Cut 12 red quilted flannel

Place line on fold

Place line on fold

**Wedge Top**

**A**
Center circle template

# I'm a Little Angel Sweatshirt

By Kate Laucomer

*Dress your own little angel in this sweatshirt of the season.*

## Project Specifications

**Skill Level:** Beginner

**Project Size:** Size varies

## Materials

- 1 child-size red sweatshirt
- Scraps green and cream prints
- 1/2 yard green print
- Red all-purpose thread
- Variegated rayon thread
- 1/8 yard fusible transfer web
- 1/4 yard tear-off fabric stabilizer
- 7 (3/4") white star buttons
- 2 (1/2") white star buttons
- Basic sewing supplies and tools

## Instructions

**Step 1.** Wash and dry sweatshirt; do not use fabric softener.

**Step 2.** Carefully remove all ribbing at neck, cuffs and waist of sweatshirt. *Note: It is easier to undo the stitching than to cut off these areas. Be careful not to stretch the neckline.*

**Step 3.** Prepare 2 yards 3"-wide bias binding from green print referring to the General Instructions.

**Step 4.** Measure around the neckline of the sweatshirt; add 1/2". Cut a piece of bias binding this length; join on short ends to make a tube.

**Step 5.** Press tube in half with wrong sides together as shown in Figure 1.

**Figure 1**
Press tube in half with wrong
sides together as shown.

**Step 6.** Evenly space and pin bias tube to right side of neck edge; sew all around using a 1/2" seam allowance. ***Note:*** *Before the next step, try the sweatshirt on the child, if possible, to be sure the neck opening is large enough.*

**Step 7.** Trim the green fabric in the seam allowance to 1/4"; turn binding to the wrong side. Hand-stitch in place.

**Step 8.** Trim length of sweatshirt at this time to make a shorter shirt, if desired.

**Step 9.** Measure around sweatshirt bottom edge; add 1/2" to this measurement. Prepare a bias tube as in Steps 4 and 5.

**Step 10.** Pin the tube right sides together with the bottom edge of the sweatshirt; sew using a 1/2" seam allowance.

**Step 11.** Turn to wrong side; hand-stitch in place.

**Step 12.** Trim sleeves to desired length. Measure cuff edge and add 1/2" to the measurement.

**Step 13.** Cut two strips green print 3 1/2" by the measurement in Step 12 for cuffs.

**Step 14.** Sew the short ends of one strip with right sides together to make a tube. Press tube in half with wrong sides together; repeat for second cuff piece.

**I'm a Little Angel Sweatshirt**
Placement Diagram
Size Varies

**Step 15.** Pin tube to the wrong side of the sweatshirt; sew. Turn over seam to the right side to create the cuff; press in place.

**Step 16.** Sew each 1/2" white star button in place on upper edge of cuff to hold in place.

**Step 17.** Trace angel parts onto the paper side of the fusible transfer web. Cut out shapes, leaving a margin around each one. ***Note:*** *To avoid the darker sweatshirt showing through lighter fabrics, you may want to fuse two layers of lighter fabrics together before tracing shapes. Treat like one layer of fabric when cutting.*

**Step 18.** Fuse shapes to the wrong side of fabrics as directed on pattern. Cut out shapes on traced lines; remove paper backing.

**Step 19.** Position the angel shapes on the center front of the sweatshirt referring to the Placement Diagram for positioning suggestions. Fuse shapes in place in numerical order.

**Step 20.** Pin tear-off fabric stabilizer behind fused shapes. Using variegated rayon thread in the top of the machine and all-purpose thread in the bobbin, machine satin-stitch around each shape. When stitching is complete, tear off stabilizer.

**Step 21.** Arrange 3/4" white star buttons around appliquéd shape. Hand-stitch in place to finish. ❧

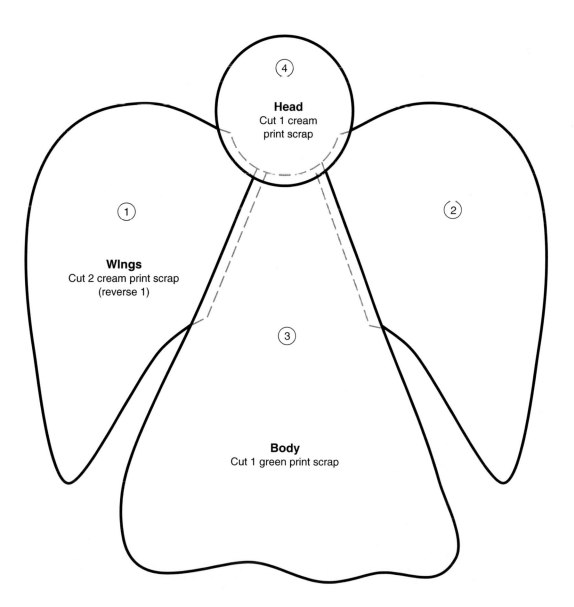

# Angel Messenger

By Kate Laucomer

*A simple Biblical message is embroidered and paired with an appliquéd angel to make this folk-art Christmas hanging.*

## Project Specifications

**Skill Level:** Beginner
**Project Size:** 13 1/2" x 19"

## Materials

- Scraps tan check, green plaid and white-on-white print
- 1/8 yard red check
- 3/8 yard green check
- 1/2 yard tan or tea-dyed muslin
- Backing 17" x 23"
- Batting 17" x 23"
- All-purpose thread to match fabrics
- 1/8 yard fusible transfer web
- Olive green 6-strand embroidery floss
- Basic sewing supplies and tools and large sheet of paper

## Instructions

**Step 1.** Cut a piece of tan or tea-dyed muslin 14" x 19".

**Step 2.** Transfer embroidery design to fabric referring to the General Instructions, placing the first word, Behold, about 7" from top edge and 4 1/2" from side edge as shown in Figure 1.

**Step 3.** Embroider each letter using 2 strands olive green embroidery floss and a backstitch as shown in Figure 2.

**Step 4.** Prepare a paper pattern for background shape referring to Figure 3, adding a 1/4" seam allowance all around when trimming pattern. Cut embroidered background to shape of pattern.

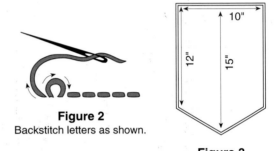

**Figure 2**
Backstitch letters as shown.

**Figure 3**
Prepare a paper pattern for background shape; add a 1/4" seam allowance all around.

**Step 5.** Trace angel shapes on the paper side of the fusible transfer web; cut out shapes leaving a margin around each one.

**Step 6.** Fuse cut shapes to the wrong side of the fabric scraps as directed on pattern for color. Cut out shapes on traced lines; remove paper backing.

**Step 7.** Arrange angel pieces above message referring to the Placement Diagram and photo of project for positioning; fuse shapes in place in numerical order.

**Step 8.** Using 2 strands olive green embroidery floss, blanket-stitch around each shape referring to the General Instructions.

**Step 9.** Cut two 1" by fabric width strips red check. Sew a strip to one long side; trim excess at top even with background. Trim excess at bottom edge at an angle even with background as shown in Figure 4; repeat on opposite side.

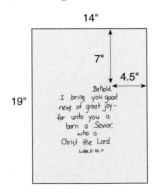

**Figure 1**
Place the first word, Behold, about 7" from top edge and 4 1/2" from side edge as shown.

**Step 10.** Sew a strip to the angled bottom edge of the background; press seam toward strip. Trim as shown in Figure 5. Sew a strip to the remaining angled bottom edge; press and trim as before. Sew a strip across top edge; press and trim.

**Figure 4**
Trim excess at bottom edge at an angle even with background.

**Figure 5**
Trim excess as shown.

**Step 11.** Cut two 2" by fabric width strips green check. Sew to background piece in the same order as the red check strips, pressing and trimming as before.

**Step 12.** Prepare project for quilting and quilt referring to the General Instructions. ***Note:** The sample quilt was hand-quilted in the ditch of each border seam and around the angel shape with thread to match fabric.*

Behold,
I bring you good
news of great joy—
for unto you is
born a Savior,
who is
Christ the Lord.

Luke 2:10, 11

**Angel Messenger**
Placement Diagram
13 1/2" x 19"

**Wing**
Cut 1 tan check

①

**Head**
Cut 1
white-on-white
print

③

**Body**
Cut 1 green plaid

②

**Step 13.** Prepare 2 yards green check bias binding and bind edges referring to the General Instructions.

**Step 14.** A sleeve may be stitched and added to the top backside referring to the General Instructions. ❧

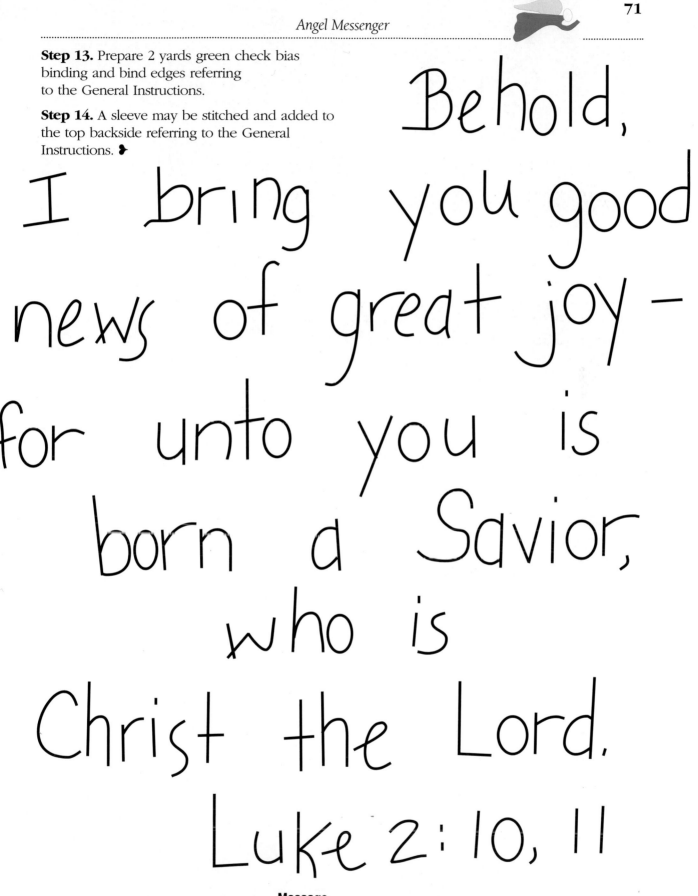

Behold, I bring you good news of great joy - for unto you is born a Savior, who is Christ the Lord.
Luke 2: 10, 11

**Message**
Backstitch each letter using 2 strands olive green embroidery floss.

# Choir of Angels

By Judith Sandstrom

*Create angel shapes using strip-pieced units in this holiday wall quilt.*

## Project Specifications

**Skill Level:** Beginner
**Project Size:** 28 1/2" x 35 1/2"
**Block Size:** 8 1/2" x 10"
**Number of Blocks:** 6

## Materials

- 1/8 yard each dark blue and cream-on-cream prints
- 1/4 yard gold print
- 3/8 yard blue plaid
- 3/8 yard red-and-blue stripe
- 5/8 yard red print
- Backing 32" x 39"
- Batting 32" x 39"
- 4 yards self-made or purchased binding
- All-purpose thread to match fabrics
- Basic sewing supplies and tools

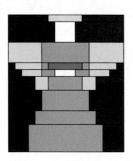

**Angel**
8 1/2" x 10" Block

## Cutting

**Step 1.** Prewash all fabrics before cutting; press.

**Step 2.** Cut one fabric-width strip red print in each of the following sizes: 2"—subcut into two 2" x 18" segments for A; 2 1/2"—subcut into four 2 1/2" x 10" strips for B; 3"—subcut into two strips 3" x 15" for C; 3 1/2"—subcut into two 3 1/2" x 8" for D, two 1 1/2" x 8" for E and two 1" x 8" for F; and 4"—subcut into two 4" x 15" strips for G.

**Step 3.** Cut one fabric-width strip blue plaid in each of the following sizes: 1 1/2"—subcut into two 1 1/2" x 8" strips for E and two 1" x 8" strips for F; 4"—subcut into two 4" x 15" strips for G; and 6"—subcut into one 6" x 18" strip for H, one 5" x 10" strip for I and one 3" x 10" strip for J.

**Step 4.** Cut one fabric-width strip gold print in each of the following sizes: 1 1/2"—subcut into two 1 1/2" x 10" strips for K; 2 1/2"—two 2 1/2" x 8" strips for L and two 2" x 8" strips for M; and 3"—subcut into one 3" x 8" strip for N and two 3" x 15" strips for C.

**Step 5.** Cut one 3" by fabric width strip dark blue print; subcut into one 3" x 8" strip for N and four 2 1/2" x 2 1/2" squares for P.

**Step 6.** Cut one 2" by fabric width strip cream-on-cream print; subcut into one 2" x 15" strip for O and one 2" x 8" strip for M.

## Piecing

***Note:*** *Sew all pieces with right sides together along length; press seams toward darkest fabrics. Subcut into segments as listed. The segments equal one row in one block.*

**Step 1.** Sew a gold N strip between two red D strips; subcut into 1" segments for Row 1 referring to Figure 1.

**Step 2.** Sew the O strip between two red print G strips; subcut into 2" segments for Row 2 referring to Figure 2.

**Figure 1**
Cut the D-N-D strip into
1" segments for Row 1.

**Figure 2**
Cut the G-O-G strip into
2" segments for Row 2.

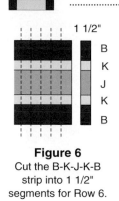

**Step 3.** Sew a blue plaid G strip between two gold C strips; subcut into 2" segments for Row 3 referring to Figure 3.

**Step 4.** Sew a red print F to L to a blue plaid F to N to a blue plaid F to L to a red print F; subcut into 1" segments for Row 4 referring to Figure 4.

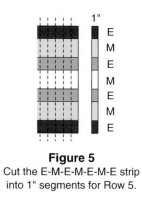

**Figure 5**
Cut the E-M-E-M-E-M-E strip into 1" segments for Row 5.

**Figure 6**
Cut the B-K-J-K-B strip into 1 1/2" segments for Row 6.

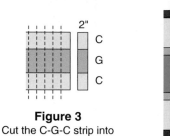

**Figure 3**
Cut the C-G-C strip into 2" segments for Row 3.

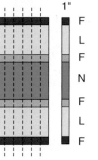

**Figure 4**
Cut the F-L-F-N-F-L-F strip into 1" segments for Row 4.

**Step 5.** Sew a red E to gold M to blue plaid E to cream M to blue plaid E to gold M to red E; subcut into 1" segments for Row 5 referring to Figure 5.

**Step 6.** Sew B to K to J to K to B; subcut into 1 1/2" segments for Row 6 referring to Figure 6.

**Step 7.** Sew C to blue plaid G to C; subcut into 2" segments for Row 7 referring to Figure 7.

**Step 8.** Sew B to I to B; subcut into 1 1/2" segments for Row 8 referring to Figure 8.

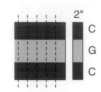

**Figure 7**
Cut the C-G-C strip into
2" segments for Row 7.

**Figure 8**
Cut the B-I-B strip
into 1 1/2" segments
for Row 8.

**Step 9.** Sew A to H to A; subcut into 2 1/2" segments for Row 9 referring to Figure 9.

**Step 10.** Arrange the rows in numerical order; join to complete one block. Repeat for six blocks.

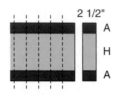

**Figure 9**
Cut the A-H-A strip
into 2 1/2" segments
for Row 9.

**Step 11.** Cut eight short sashing strips 2" x 10 1/2" and three long sashing strips 2" x 32" red print.

**Step 12.** Join four blocks and four short sashing strips to make a row beginning and ending with a sashing strip; repeat for two rows.

**Step 13.** Join the two rows with three long sashing strips as shown in Figure 10.

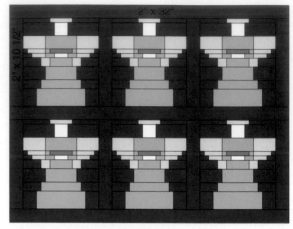

**Figure 10**
Join the 2 rows with 3 long sashing strips.

**Step 14.** Cut two strips each 2 1/2" x 25" and 2 1/2" x 32" red-and-blue stripe. Sew the longer strips to opposite long sides. Sew a P square to the end of each shorter strip and sew to the remaining sides to complete the pieced top.

**Step 15.** Prepare quilt for quilting; quilt and finish referring to the General Instructions. ❥

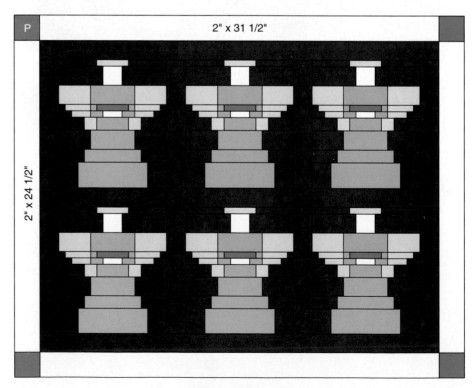

**Choir of Angels**
Placement Diagram
28 1/2" x 35 1/2"

# Festive Holly Place Mats & Napkin Rings

By Karen Neary

*Try a new shape for your holiday place mats using the simple holly-leaf shape to create the design.*

## Project Specifications

Skill Level: Intermediate

Place Mat Size: 15 1/2" x 18" (includes binding)

Napkin: 19" x 19"

Napkin Ring: 1 1/2" diameter

## Materials

(For 4 place mats and napkins)

- 1/4 yard red mottled
- 1/2 yard green print
- 1 yard backing fabric
- 2 1/8 yards gold/cream stripe
- 1 yard quilter's fleece
- 8 yards self-made or purchased red bias binding
- Cream, red and green all-purpose thread
- 1 1/2 yards fusible transfer web
- 2 yards tear-off fabric stabilizer
- Basic sewing supplies and tools, large sheet of paper and water-erasable marker

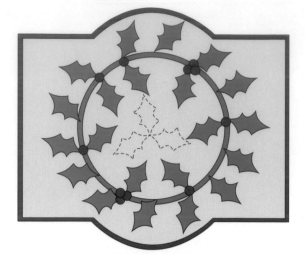

**Festive Holly Place Mat**
Placement Diagram
15 1/2" x 18"
(includes binding)

**Festive Holly Napkin Ring**
Placement Diagram
1 1/2" diameter

## Place Mat

**Step 1.** Prepare templates using patterns given. Cut as directed on Place Mat Background for one place mat; repeat for four place mats.

**Step 2.** Bond fusible transfer web to the wrong side of the green and red fabrics. Fold large sheet of paper in half; fold in half again. Trace pattern for Holly Wreath as shown in Figure 1. Trace four wreath shapes on fused fabric.

**Figure 1**
Trace pattern for Holly Wreath
on paper as shown.

**Step 3.** Trace leaves and berries on fused fabrics as directed on each piece for one place mat; repeat for four place mats. Cut out shapes on traced lines; remove paper backing.

**Step 4.** Transfer the inside line of the wreath shape onto the center of one gold/cream background piece using a water-erasable marker.

**Step 5.** Pin the wreath shape on the marked line on the place mat top referring to Figure 2; fuse in place.

**Step 6.** Pin tear-off fabric stabilizer to the wrong side of the place mat. Using green all-purpose thread, machine satin-stitch around both edges of the wreath shape.

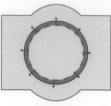

**Figure 2**
Pin the wreath shape on the
marked line as shown.

**Step 7.** Arrange the holly leaves and berries around the wreath shape referring to the Placement Diagram for positioning of pieces; fuse shapes in place.

**Step 8.** Appliqué in place as in Step 6 using thread to match the fabrics. Remove the stabilizer when appliqué is complete.

**Step 9.** Sandwich quilter's fleece between the appliquéd top and backing pieces; pin or baste layers together. Machine-quilt around holly leaves and wreath using cream all-purpose thread. Mark a few holly leaves in the center and machine-quilt.

**Step 10.** Remove pins or basting and bind edges with self-made or purchased red bias binding referring to the General Instructions.

## Napkin & Napkin Ring

**Step 1.** Cut one 20" x 20" square gold/cream stripe for each napkin.

**Step 2.** Turn under each side of each napkin 1/4" twice for hem. Stitch using cream all-purpose thread.

**Step 3.** For each napkin ring, cut a 2 1/2" x 6" rectangle green print. Fold along length with right sides together; stitch along length. Turn right side out; press with seam on edge.

**Step 4.** Sew short ends together to form a circle using a 1/8" seam allowance; turn and sew right sides together again using a 1/4" seam allowance to form a French seam and enclose raw edges.

**Step 5.** Layer two scraps of green print wrong sides together with quilter's fleece between. Trace holly pattern on fabric and straight-stitch on marked line. Trim outside edges just beyond stitching.

**Step 6.** With tear-off fabric stabilizer under the cut leaves, machine zigzag-stitch around outside

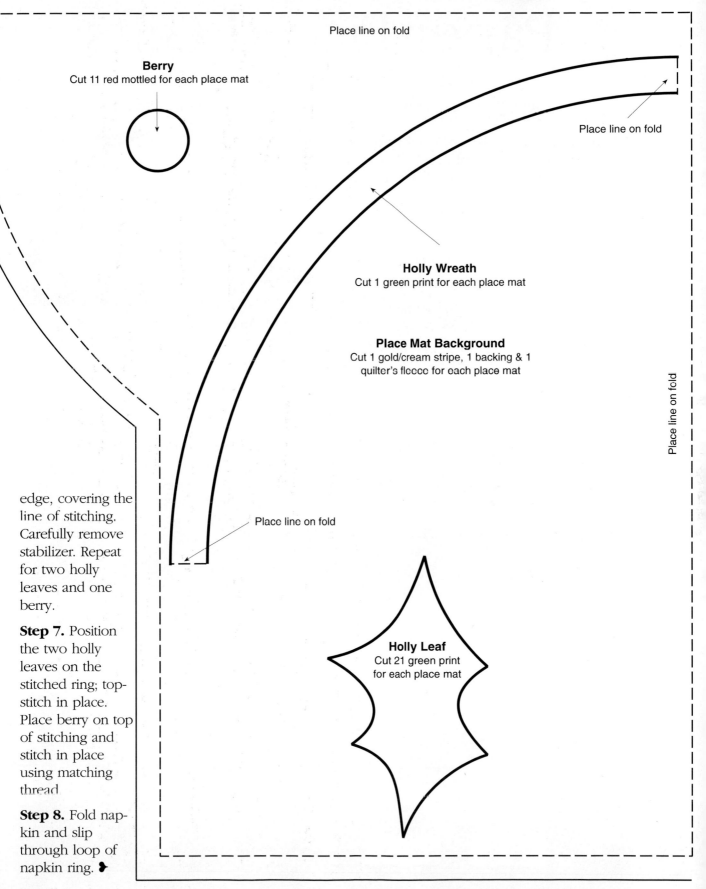

Place line on fold

**Berry**
Cut 11 red mottled for each place mat

Place line on fold

**Holly Wreath**
Cut 1 green print for each place mat

**Place Mat Background**
Cut 1 gold/cream stripe, 1 backing & 1
quilter's fleece for each place mat

Place line on fold

Place line on fold

edge, covering the line of stitching. Carefully remove stabilizer. Repeat for two holly leaves and one berry.

**Step 7.** Position the two holly leaves on the stitched ring; top-stitch in place. Place berry on top of stitching and stitch in place using matching thread.

**Step 8.** Fold napkin and slip through loop of napkin ring. ❧

**Holly Leaf**
Cut 21 green print
for each place mat

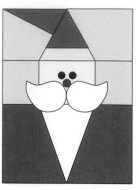

# Paper-Pieced Gifts

By Chris Malone

*Paper-pieced cards or tree ornaments are fun to stitch and make great gifts.*

For each pattern, trace or copy all of the lines and numbers onto a piece of plain paper. If desired, enlarge or reduce patterns with a copy machine. The numbers indicate the order in which each piece is sewn. The fabric pieces do not have to be cut precisely, but should be large enough to completely cover the numbered area and extend at least 1/4" beyond the seam line on all sides.

The fabric is held on the bottom or unprinted side of the paper; sewing is done on the printed side of the paper, directly on the lines through paper and fabric.

When all seams are completed, the paper is torn away. Set the sewing machine to a stitch length of 12–15 stitches per inch so the stitching is secure and the paper tears away more easily.

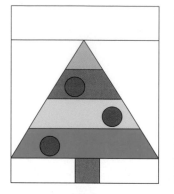

**Tree**
3 3/4" x 4 1/2" Block

**Santa**
3 3/4" x 5" Block

## Tree Mini Banner

### Project Specifications

Skill Level: Intermediate

Project Size: 5 3/4" x 6 1/2"

Block Size: 3 3/4" x 4 1/2"

Number of Blocks: 1

### Materials

- Scraps of 4 green prints, brown print and white print
- 1/4 yard red print
- Low-loft batting 6" x 7"
- Neutral color all-purpose thread
- Ecru quilting thread
- 3 (1/2") and 2 (5/8") red buttons
- 1" wooden star button
- Gold acrylic paint and paintbrush
- Black fine-line permanent marking pen
- Basic sewing supplies and tools and tweezers

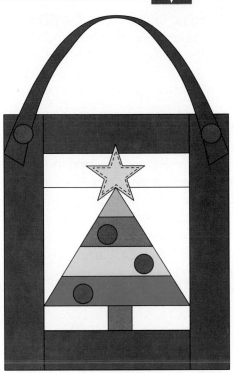

**Tree Mini Banner**
Placement Diagram
5 3/4" x 6 1/2"

## Instructions

**Step 1.** Center selected fabric right side up over section 1 on the unmarked side of the paper. Hold the paper up to a light to make sure that the edges of the fabric extend at least 1/4" beyond the seam line on all sides. Pin the piece in place; place the fabric for piece 2 right sides together with piece one, checking piece 2 as you did piece 1 for size.

**Step 2.** Turn paper over and sew on the line between pieces 1 and 2, extending the sewing 2–3 stitches beyond the line at the beginning and end as shown in Figure 1.

**Step 3.** Trim excess seam to 1/4". Fold piece 2 back, right side up and press. Repeat with all pieces in numerical order.

**Figure 1**
Sew on the line between piece 1 and 2, extending the sewing 2–3 stitches beyond the line at the beginning and end.

**Step 4.** Trim block along solid outer line.

**Step 5.** Cut two strips each 1 1/2" x 4 1/4" and 1 1/2" x 7" red print. Sew the shorter strips to the top and bottom, sewing on the inner border line of the paper pattern. Sew remaining strips to sides of block; press seams toward strips. Carefully remove the paper backing, one section at a time, using tweezers if necessary.

**Step 6.** Cut a red print backing piece using the pieced top as a pattern. Place the batting piece on a flat surface; lay backing right side up on top of batting. Place the block right side down on the backing; pin layers together.

**Step 7.** Sew all around, leaving a 3" opening at center bottom. Trim batting close to seam and clip corners. Turn right side out and press. Fold in seam allowance and hand-stitch opening closed.

**Step 8.** Hand-quilt in the ditch between block and border strips using ecru quilting thread.

**Step 9.** For hanger, cut one 2" x 12" strip red print. Fold in half along length with right sides together; sew along all raw edges, leaving a 2" opening in the center. Clip corners and turn right side out; press with seam on edge. Hand-stitch the opening closed.

**Step 10.** Hand-stitch a few gathering stitches

1 3/4"

**Figure 2**
Hand-stitch a few gathering stitches across each end of the strip 1 3/4" from ends.

*The Christmas Home*

across each end of the strip 1 3/4" from ends as shown in Figure 2. Pull tightly.

**Step 11.** Place gathered area on one corner of mini quilt; sew a 5/8" red button to hanger and mini quilt to attach hanger to quilt. Repeat on the opposite corner.

**Step 12.** Paint wooden star button with gold acrylic paint; recoat as necessary. Use black fine-line permanent marking pen to draw short straight lines resembling stitches along edges. Sew to quilt at top of tree. Sew 1/2" red buttons to tree referring to the photo of the project for positioning suggestions.

## Santa Card

### Project Specifications

Skill Level: Intermediate

Project Size: 5" x 7"

Block Size: 3 3/4" x 5"

Number of Blocks: 1

### Materials

- Scraps of tan solid and red, cream and 2 tan prints
- Quilter's fleece 4 1/2" x 6"
- Neutral color all-purpose thread
- 1 1/2" x 3" piece fusible transfer web
- 2 (5mm) black half beads
- 6mm wooden half bead
- Red acrylic paint and paintbrush
- 2 sheets red card stock
- 1/2" tan button
- Permanent fabric adhesive
- Basic sewing supplies and tools, craft knife and tweezers

## Instructions

**Step 1.** Paper-piece sections 1–4 for Santa referring to Project Notes and Steps 1–3 for Tree Mini Banner. Join sections as shown in Figure 3.

**Step 2.** With paper side up, sew all around completed block on inner border line; trim block on outer solid line. Carefully remove paper backing, one section at a time, using tweezers, if necessary.

**Step 3.** Cut one sheet of card stock 7" x 10". Fold in half so card measures 5" x 7" and crease.

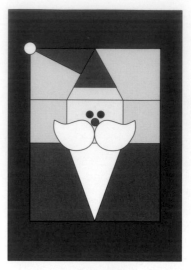

**Santa Card**
Placement Diagram
5" x 7"

**Step 4.** Measure block from outer stitched lines and cut out an equal size opening on one half of the folded card. **Note:** *All of the design should show through the opening but stitched lines should be just under the edge.* Apply permanent fabric adhesive to inside edge of card

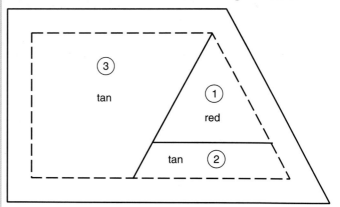

**Santa Pattern Section 1**

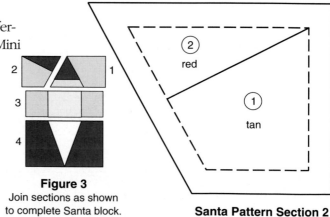

**Santa Pattern Section 2**

**Figure 3**
Join sections as shown
to complete Santa block.

opening; insert block and press to set.

**Step 5.** Place quilter's fleece rectangle on inside of card against the wrong side of the block. Cut a 5" x 7" piece from the remaining sheet of card stock; glue to inside of card, covering fleece.

**Step 6.** Prepare a template for the mustache piece using pattern given. Trace shape on the paper side of the fusible transfer web referring to the pattern for cutting instructions. Cut out shapes, leaving a margin around each one; remove paper backing. Fuse shapes to the wrong side of the tan scrap. ***Note:*** *Use the same scrap as was used to make beard area in Section 3.*

**Step 7.** Fuse two mustache pieces together to make a heavier shape. Using permanent fabric adhesive, glue shapes to face area referring to the Placement Diagram for positioning, leaving tips of mustache loose.

**Step 8.** Paint the 6mm wooden half bead with red acrylic paint; glue to center of face area. ***Note:*** *Place bead on a piece of doubled tape to hold while painting.* Glue black half beads to face area for eyes. Glue 1/2" tan button to corner of card opening at top of hat to finish. ❧

**Mustache**
Cut 4 tan scrap
(reverse half)

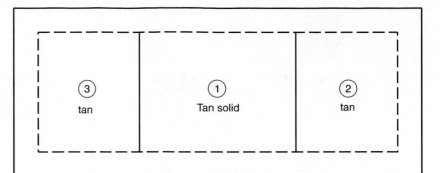

**Santa Pattern Section 3**

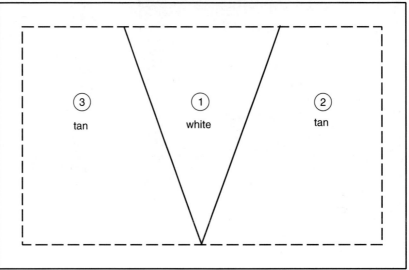

**Santa Pattern Section 4**

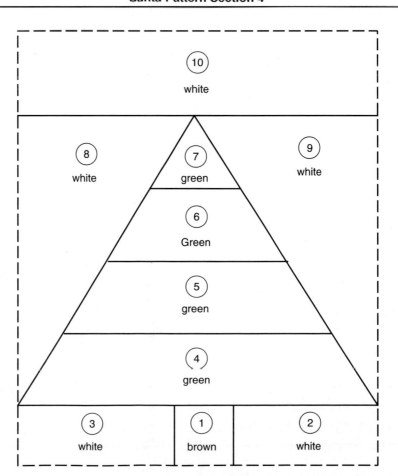

**Tree Pattern**

# We Three Kings

By Judith Sandstrom

*Tiny pieces are used to create this pieced design. Each king wears a different color turban and robe.*

## Project Specifications

**Skill Level:** Intermediate

**Project Size:** 22" x 22 1/2"

**Blocks Size:** 4 1/2" x 16"

**Number of Blocks:** 3

## Materials

- Scraps muslin and brown print
- 1/8 yard total 9 colorful scraps for turbans and robes
- 1/8 yard gold print
- 1/4 yard multicolored print
- 3/8 yard navy print
- Backing 26" x 26"
- Batting 26" x 26"
- Neutral color all-purpose thread
- Basic sewing supplies and tools

## Instructions

**Note:** *The block is pieced in rows. Seams in each row are pressed toward the darkest fabric. Row 1 is the same in all blocks; all other rows are specific to each block. Fabrics in these rows are referred to as the item being pieced, for example, turban, robe and turban/sleeve. Use the same fabric for the item within a block but different fabrics for the item in the other blocks.*

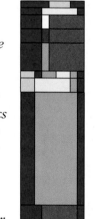

**We Three Kings**
4 1/2" x 16" Block

**Step 1.** For Row 1, cut one rectangle each 2 1/2" x 5" navy print, 2" x 5" gold print and 1 1/2" x 5" navy print. Join the pieces in the order given; subcut into three 1" segments for Row 1 as shown in Figure 1.

**Step 2.** For Row 2, cut one each 2" x 2" navy print, 3" x 2" turban/sleeve scrap and 1" x 2"

navy print. Join the pieces in the order given; cut into a 1" segment to complete one Row 2 as shown in Figure 2. Repeat for three rows.

**Figure 1**
Make Row 1 as shown.

**Figure 2**
Make Row 2 as shown.

**Step 3.** For Row 3, cut one each 2" x 2" navy print, 1" x 2" muslin scrap and 3" x 2" turban scrap. Join the pieces in the order given; cut into a 1 1/2" segment to complete one Row 3 as shown in Figure 3. Repeat for three rows.

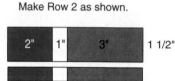

**Figure 3**
Make Row 3 as shown.

**Step 4.** For Row 4, cut one each 2" x 2" navy print, 1" x 2" brown print and 3" x 2" turban scrap. Join the pieces in the order given and

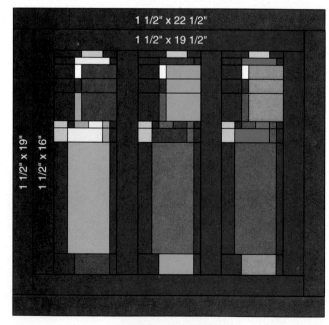

**We Three Kings**
Placement Diagram
22" x 22 1/2"

cut into a 1 1/2" segment to complete one Row 4 as shown in Figure 4. Repeat for three rows.

**Step 5.** For Row 5, cut one each 2" x 3" navy print, 1" x 3" main robe scrap and 3" x 3" turban scrap. Join the pieces in the order given and cut into a 2 1/2" segment to complete one Row 5 as shown in Figure 5. Repeat for three rows.

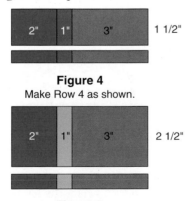

| 2" | 1" | 3" | 1 1/2" |

**Figure 4**
Make Row 4 as shown.

| 2" | 1" | 3" | 2 1/2" |

**Figure 5**
Make Row 5 as shown.

**Step 6.** For Row 6, cut one each 1 1/2" x 2" gold print, 1" x 2" navy print, 1 1/2" x 2" main robe scrap, 1 1/2" x 2" turban/sleeve scrap, 1" x 2" main robe scrap and 1" x 2" navy print. Join the pieces in the order given and cut into a 1" segment to complete one Row 6 as shown in Figure 6. Repeat for three rows.

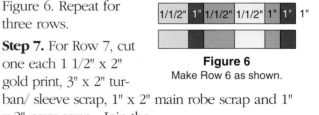

| 1/1/2" | 1" | 1/1/2" | 1/1/2" | 1" | 1" | 1" |

**Figure 6**
Make Row 6 as shown.

**Step 7.** For Row 7, cut one each 1 1/2" x 2" gold print, 3" x 2" turban/ sleeve scrap, 1" x 2" main robe scrap and 1" x 2" navy scrap . Join the pieces in the order given and cut into a 1 1/2" segment to complete one Row 7 as shown in Figure 7. Repeat for three rows.

| 1 1/2" | 3" | 1" | 1" | 1 1/2" |

**Figure 7**
Make Row 7 as shown.

**Step 8.** For Row 8, cut one each 1 1/2" x 9" navy print, 3 1/2" x 9" main robe scrap and 1" x 9" navy print. Join the pieces in the order given and

*We Three Kings continued on page 87*

*The Christmas Home*

# Melt-Your-Heart Snowman Card Holder

By Chris Malone

*You won't have to look far to find your cards and letters if you place them in the pockets of this simple appliquéd card holder.*

---

### Project Specifications

**Skill Level:** Beginner
**Project Size:** Approximately 16" x 36"

---

### Materials

- Scraps red and green checks and white-on-white, brown, orange and red prints or solids
- 10 1/2" x 10 1/2" square blue print
- 1/8 yard gold print
- 5/8 yard green print
- 1 yard red print
- Batting 18" x 38"
- All-purpose thread to match fabrics
- Blue, gold and green or black quilting thread
- Black, brown and white 6-strand embroidery floss
- 1/4 yard lightweight fusible transfer web
- 2 (6mm) black half beads
- 3 (5/8") and 2 (1") black buttons
- 2 (2 7/8") wooden stars
- 4 (1") wooden star buttons
- 1" x 20" wooden slat
- 2 small sawtooth hangers
- Gold acrylic paint and paintbrush
- Wood stain
- Black fine-line permanent marking pen
- Matte spray finish
- Permanent adhesive
- No-fray solution
- Air-erasable pen
- Basic sewing supplies and tools, rotary cutter, mat and ruler

---

## Instructions

**Step 1.** Trace all appliqué pieces onto the paper side of the lightweight fusible transfer web; cut just outside traced lines.

**Melt-Your-Heart Snowman Card Holder**
Placement Diagram
Approximately 16" x 36"

**Figure 1**
Make stem stitch as shown.

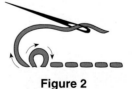

**Figure 2**
Make a backstitch as shown.

**Step 2.** Referring to the manufacturer's instructions, fuse traced shapes to the wrong side of fabrics as indicated on patterns for color. Cut out shapes on traced lines; remove paper backing.

**Step 3.** Center and arrange pieces on the 10 1/2" x 10 1/2" square blue print in numerical order; fuse shapes in place.

**Step 4.** Using black quilting thread for machine appliqué or 2 strands of black embroidery floss for hand appliqué, blanket-stitch around each shape except the hatband by hand or machine referring to the General Instructions.

**Step 5.** Lightly mark twig arms with air-erasable pen; stem-stitch over lines with 2 strands brown embroidery floss referring to Figure 1.

**Step 6.** Mark smile and backstitch using 2 strands black embroidery floss referring to Figure 2. Make two straight stitches for eyebrows. Backstitch line between twig arm and heart using 2 strands white embroidery floss.

**Step 7.** Cut two strips each 1 1/2" x 10 1/2" and 1 1/2" x 12 1/2" gold print. Sew the shorter strips to the top and bottom and the longer strips to opposite sides of the appliquéd square; press seams toward strips.

**Step 8.** Cut three 2 1/2" x 12 1/2" and two 2 1/2" x 40" strips red print. Sew the shorter strips to the top and bottom of the appliquéd square; press seams toward strips. Set the longer strips aside.

**Step 9.** Cut one 12 1/2" x 20" and four 12 1/2" x 6 1/4" rectangles green print. Sew longer strip to the bottom of

**Figure 3**
Place first pocket strip across green section with hemmed top at seam line as shown.

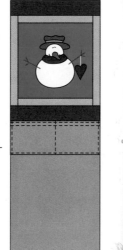

**Figure 4**
Sew a second seam 3/8" up, encasing raw edge in seam. Sew a scant 1/4" seam at sides. Sew down center of strip to make 2 pockets.

the stitched unit; press seam toward green print rectangle. *Note: This piece and the two long red print border strips are cut slightly long and will be trimmed later to allow for individual differences in piecing.*

**Step 10.** To make card pockets, fold and press a double 1/2" hem along one long edge of each green print rectangle for top edge of pocket. Topstitch in two rows 1/4" apart. Turn under remaining long edge 1/4"; press. Place first pocket strip across green section with hemmed top at seam line as shown in Figure 3; pin. Sew across bottom close to fold; sew a second seam 3/8" up, encasing raw edge in seam, referring to Figure 4; sew a scant 1/4" seam at sides. Sew down center of strip to make two pockets, again referring to Figure 4.

**Step 11.** Place a second pocket strip across the green print section, overlapping first pocket

5/8" as shown in Figure 5; pin. Sew in place as for first pocket; repeat with remaining two strips. Trim bottom green section so a generous seam allowance of 5/16" remains below bottom of last row of pockets as shown in Figure 6.

**Step 12.** Sew the long red print strips cut in Step 8 to opposite long sides of the pieced section; trim excess and press seams toward strips. Sew the remaining shorter strip to the bottom; press seams toward strips.

**Step 13.** Cut a piece of red print backing and batting using the pieced top as a pattern.

**Step 14.** Place batting on a flat surface; lay backing piece right side up on top of batting. Place the pieced-and-appliquéd top right sides together with the backing piece; pin layers together to secure.

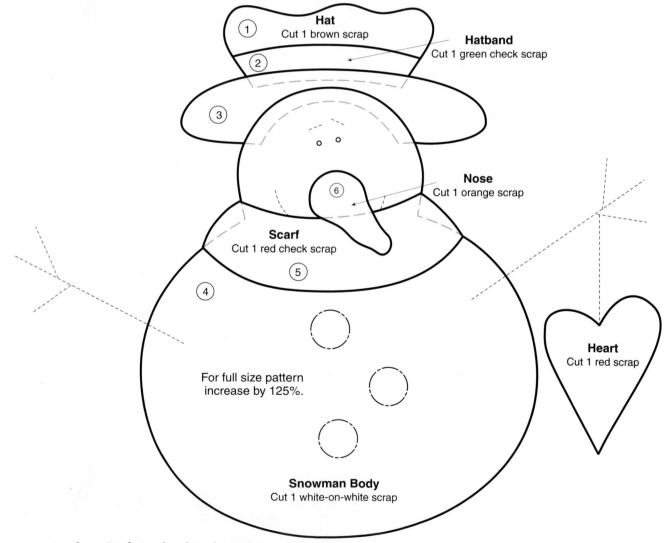

**Hat**
Cut 1 brown scrap
① ②

**Hatband**
Cut 1 green check scrap

③

**Nose**
Cut 1 orange scrap
⑥

**Scarf**
Cut 1 red check scrap
⑤

④

For full size pattern increase by 125%.

**Heart**
Cut 1 red scrap

**Snowman Body**
Cut 1 white-on-white scrap

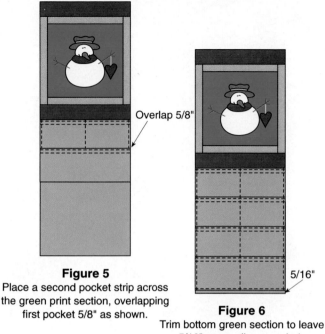

**Figure 5**
Place a second pocket strip across
the green print section, overlapping
first pocket 5/8" as shown.

**Figure 6**
Trim bottom green section to leave
a 5/16" seam allowance below
bottom of last pocket as shown.

**Step 15.** Stitch around all sides leaving a 6" opening at the center bottom. Trim batting close to seam; clip corners. Turn right side out through opening; press. Hand-stitch opening closed.

**Step 16.** Using matching color quilting thread, hand- or machine-quilt in the ditch of seams between all strips and the appliquéd block.

**Step 17.** Cut two 4 1/2" x 8 1/2" strips green print for hanging loops. Fold each strip in half along length with right sides together; sew all edges, leaving a 2" opening. Clip corners and turn right side out. Press; hand-stitch opening closed.

**Step 18.** Fold each loop over top of wall quilt overlapping top about 1 1/4" on front and back and in about 3" from each side. Sew 1" black button to top of loops, sewing through all layers to secure.

**Step 19.** Glue black half beads to snowman's face for eyes. For scarf, cut 3/4" x 6" strip red check. Fringe short ends 1/2" and apply no-fray solution to long edges. When dry, tie a knot in the center of strip; glue knot to side of snowman's neck. Sew 5/8" black buttons down body of snowman referring to marks on pattern for positioning.

**Step 20.** Paint wooden stars and star buttons with gold acrylic paint. Recoat as necessary and let dry. Use the black fine-line permanent marking pen to draw short straight lines resembling stitches around all edges. Apply wood stain to slat. Spray all wooden pieces with matte finish.

**Step 21.** Sew star buttons to background around snowman using gold quilting thread. Attach sawtooth hangers to both ends on back of wooden slat. Glue large stars to front ends of slat. Slip slat through hanging loops to hang. ❧

*We Three Kings*
*Continued from page 83*

cut into an 8 1/2" segment to complete one Row 8 as shown in Figure 8. Repeat for three rows.

**Step 9.** For Row 9, cut one each 2" x 3" navy print, 3" x 3" turban scrap and 1" x 3" navy print. Join the pieces in the order given and cut into a 2" segment to complete one Row 9 as shown in Figure 9. Repeat for three rows.

**Step 10.** Sew rows 1–8 together to make a block. Repeat for 3 blocks. Cut four strips navy print 2" x 16 1/2". Join the

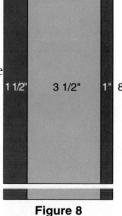

**Figure 8**
Make Row 8 as shown.

three blocks with the four strips beginning and ending with a strip; press seams toward strips.

**Step 11.** Cut two strips navy print 2" x 20"; sew to the top and bottom of the pieced top. Press seams toward strips.

**Step 12.** Cut two strips each multicolored print 2" x 19 1/2" and 2" x 23". Sew the shorter strips to opposite short sides of the pieced top and longer strips to the top and bottom; press seams toward strips.

**Step 13.** Prepare quilt for quilting; quilt and finish referring to the General Instructions. ❧

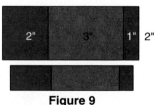

**Figure 9**
Make Row 9 as shown.

# Quick Classics

Traditional patterns are still favorites among many quilters. If you like to make quilted projects with more familiar designs, you will be thrilled with the group of projects in this chapter.

Complete your project in 20 hours or less and be prepared to start another one as soon as you finish.

Collect the materials, supplies and tools and get your sewing area ready as you prepare yourself for an inspiring sewing session.

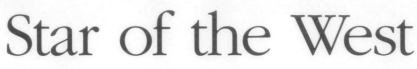

# Star of the West

By Pearl L. Krush

*A Western-theme print is featured in this pretty quilt which may be used as a centerpiece for your bed or to hang on the wall as an accent in any room.*

## Project Specifications

**Skill Level:** Beginner

**Project Size:** 62" x 62"

**Block Size:** 4" x 4", 6" x 6" and 8" x 8"

**Number of Blocks:** 4 small, 4 medium and 16 large

## Materials

- 1/2 yard brown print
- 2/3 yard each gold and blue prints
- 3/4 yard red print
- 1 yard dark blue print
- 1 2/3 yards cream-on-cream print
- Backing 66" x 66"
- Batting 66" x 66"
- 7 1/4 yards self-made or purchased binding
- All-purpose thread to match fabrics
- Basic sewing supplies and tools

**Star of the West**
Placement Diagram
62" x 62"

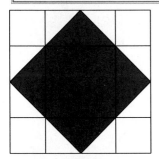

**Square-in-a-Square**
8" x 8" Block
Make 8

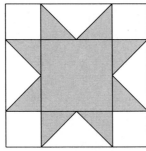

**Square and Points**
8" x 8" Block
Make 8

**Nine-Patch**
6" x 6" Block
Make 4

**Pinwheel**
4" x 4" Block
Make 4

## Instructions

**Step 1.** Cut the following fabric-width strips from the cream-on-cream print: eight 2 1/2"-wide strips—subcut into 2 1/2" square segments for 128 A squares; four 2 1/2"-wide strips—subcut into 4 1/2" segments for 32 B rectangles; one 2 7/8"-wide strip—subcut into eight 2 7/8" square segments for C; and three 6 1/2"-wide strips—set aside to cut D pieces.

**Step 2.** Cut the following fabric-width strips from blue and gold prints: one 4 1/2" strip each fabric—subcut into eight 4 1/2" square segments each for E and two 2 1/2"-wide strips each fabric—set aside for Nine-Patch blocks. Cut four 2 1/2"-wide strips blue print—subcut into 4 1/2" segments for 32 B rectangles. Cut four 2 1/2"-wide strips gold print—subcut into 2 1/2" square segments for 64 A squares.

*Quick-to-Stitch Weekend Quilts & Projects*

**Step 3.** Cut the following fabric-width strips from red print: one 2 7/8"-wide strip—subcut into eight 2 7/8" square segments for C; three 6 1/2"-wide strips—set aside to cut D pieces.

**Step 4.** Place a gold print A square on a cream-on-cream print B; stitch on the diagonal of A as shown in Figure 1. Trim seam to 1/4" as shown in Figure 2; press A to right side. Repeat with a second A on the opposite end of B to complete one B unit; repeat for 32 units.

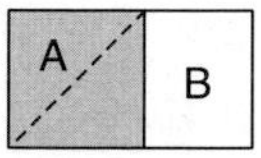

**Figure 1**
Place a gold print A square on a cream-on-cream print B; stitch on the diagonal of A.

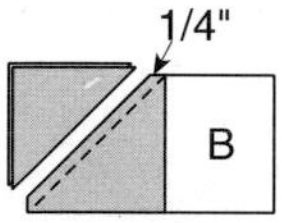

**Figure 2**
Trim seam to 1/4" as shown

**Step 5.** To piece one Square and Points block, sew a B unit to two opposite sides of a gold print E as shown in Figure 3.

**Figure 3**
Sew a B unit to 2 opposite sides of a gold print E.

**Step 6.** Sew a cream-on-cream print A to each end of two B units as shown in Figure 4; sew an A-B unit to opposite sides of the B-E unit as shown in Figure 5 to complete one Square and Points block. Repeat for eight blocks.

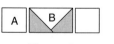

**Figure 4**
Sew a cream-on-cream print A to each end of 2 B units.

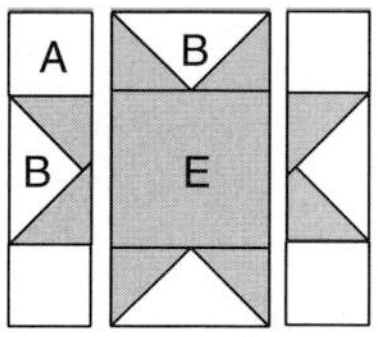

**Figure 5**
Sew an A-B unit to opposite sides of the B-E unit as shown to complete 1 Square and Points block.

**Step 7.** To make one Square-in-a-Square block, use the blue print B and E pieces and cream-on-cream print A squares and refer to Steps 4–6 and Figure 6 to complete one block; repeat for eight blocks.

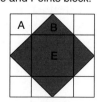

**Figure 6**
Use the blue print B and E pieces and cream-on-cream print A squares to complete 1 Square-in-a-Square block.

**Step 8.** Cut one strip brown print 2 1/2" by fabric width; subcut into 2 1/2" square segments to make nine sashing squares.

**Step 9.** Cut five strips dark blue print 2 1/2" by fabric width; subcut into 8 1/2" segments to make 24 sashing strips.

**Step 10.** Join four sashing strips and three sashing squares to make a sashing row; press seams toward strips. Repeat for three sashing rows.

**Step 11.** Join two Square and Points blocks and two Square-in-a-Square blocks with three sashing strips to make a block row as shown in Figure 7; press seams toward strips. Repeat for four block rows.

2 1/2" x 8 1/2"

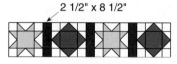

**Figure 7**
Join 2 Square and Points blocks and 2 Square-in-a-Square blocks with 3 sashing strips to make a block row.

**Step 12.** Join the block rows and the sashing rows to complete the pieced center referring to the Placement Diagram for positioning of rows; press seams in one direction.

**Step 13.** To make Pinwheel blocks, place a red print C square right sides together with a cream-on-cream print C square. Draw a diagonal line on the lighter square.

**Step 14.** Sew 1/4" from each side of the drawn line; cut apart on the drawn line as shown in Figure 8 to make triangle/square units. Repeat for 16 units.

**Step 15.** Join four units as shown in Figure 9 to make a Pinwheel block; repeat for four blocks.

1/4"

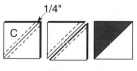

**Figure 8**
Sew 1/4" on each side of the drawn line; cut apart on the drawn line as shown to make triangle/square units.

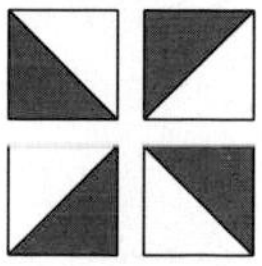

**Figure 9**
Join 4 units as shown to make a Pinwheel block.

**Step 16.** Cut four strips dark blue print 4 1/2" x 38 1/2". Sew a strip to opposite sides of the pieced center; press seams toward strips.

**Step 17.** Sew a Pinwheel block to each end of the remaining two strips; sew these strips to the remaining sides of the pieced center. Press seams toward strips.

**Step 18.** Cut and piece two strips each 2 1/2" x 46 1/2" and 2 1/2" x 50 1/2" brown print; sew shorter strips to opposite sides and longer strips to the top and bottom. Press seams toward strips.

**Step 19.** Prepare template for D using pattern given. Place one 6 1/2"-wide strip each cream-on-cream and red prints with right sides together; pin. Place the D template on the pinned strips as shown in Figure 10; trace and cut as directed on D.

**Step 20.** Sew a red print D to a cream-on-cream print D as shown in Figure 11; repeat with DR pieces. You will need 24 of each unit.

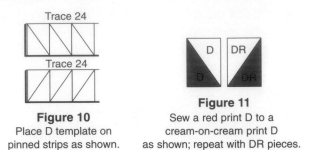

**Figure 10**
Place D template on pinned strips as shown.

**Figure 11**
Sew a red print D to a cream-on-cream print D as shown; repeat with DR pieces.

**Step 21.** Join six each D and DR units to make a strip as shown in Figure 12; repeat for four strips.

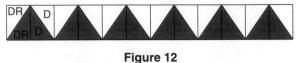

**Figure 12**
Join 6 each D and DR units to make a strip.

**Step 22.** Cut the remaining 2 1/2"-wide gold and blue print strips into 2 1/2" x 21" strips. Sew a blue print strip between two gold print strips with right sides together along length. Repeat with a gold print strip between two blue print strips. Subcut strip sets into 2 1/2" segments.

**Step 23.** Join two gold/blue/gold segments with one blue/gold/blue segment to make a Nine-Patch block as shown in Figure 13; repeat for four blocks.

**Figure 13**
Join 2 gold/blue/gold segments with 1 blue/gold/blue segment to make a Nine-Patch block

**Step 24.** Sew a D/DR strip to opposite sides of the pieced center; press seams toward strips. Sew a Nine-Patch block to each end of the remaining two D/DR strips and sew to the remaining sides of the pieced center; press seams toward strips.

**Step 25.** Prepare for quilting, quilt and bind referring to the General Instructions. ***Note:*** *The quilt shown was machine-quilted in a meandering design using all-purpose thread to match fabrics.* ❥

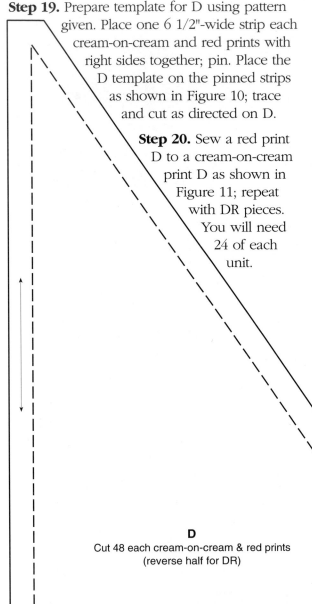

**D**
Cut 48 each cream-on-cream & red prints
(reverse half for DR)

# A Touch of Patchwork

By Joyce Livingston

*Dress up that blue denim shirt with a few plaid scraps and your
one-of-a-kind shirt will bring compliments galore.*

## Project Specifications

**Skill Level:** Beginner
**Shirt Size:** Size varies
**Block Size:** 4" x 4"
**Number of Blocks:** 7

## Materials

- Variety of dark and light plaid scraps
- Adult-size denim shirt with pockets and back yoke
- All-purpose thread to match fabrics
- Freezer paper
- Basic sewing supplies and tools and yarn or string

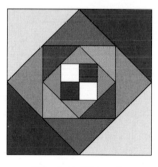

**Monkey Wrench**
4" x 4" Block

Although the shirt used has a back yoke with two front pockets, the paper-pieced blocks may be joined as a unit and appliquéd to almost any area on a shirt, with or without a yoke. Use the instructions provided to create the blocks and apply them to the shirt as shown in the sample. Make adjustments as necessary to fit the style shirt and as to the number of blocks needed, as shirt size will vary.

## Instructions

**Step 1.** Cut one strip each light and dark plaid scraps 1" x 16". Join the strips with right sides

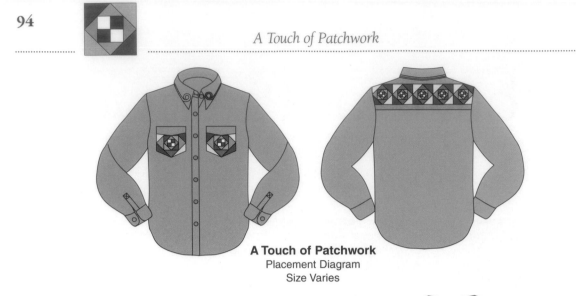

**A Touch of Patchwork**
Placement Diagram
Size Varies

together along length; subcut into 1" segments. Join two segments to make a Four-Patch unit as shown in Figure 1; repeat for seven Four-Patch units for the block centers.

**Step 2.** Make copies of the paper-piecing pattern using pattern given. Transfer lines to the wrong side of the paper. Pin a Four-Patch unit right side up on the wrong side of the paper over the center area as shown in Figure 2.

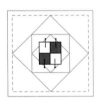

**Figure 1**
Join 2 segments to make a Four-Patch unit.

**Figure 2**
Pin a Four-Patch unit right side up on the wrong side of the paper over the center area as shown.

**Step 3.** Cut scrap fabrics to fit numbered areas in the pattern, adding a seam allowance and referring to the General Instructions and page 17.

**Step 4.** Sew pieces to paper foundation in numerical order, again referring to the General Instructions for paper-piecing specifics. Complete seven blocks.

**Step 5.** To create a paper pattern for the shirt yoke and pockets, iron pieces of freezer paper with the shiny side down onto the yoke and one pocket to make it adhere to the fabric. This will leave the impression of the yoke and pocket on the paper. Pull the paper off and add a 1/4" seam all around; cut out to make patterns as shown in Figure 3.

**Figure 3**
Pull the paper off and add a 1/4" seam all around; cut out to make patterns as shown.

**Step 6.** To assemble yoke, join five blocks to make a strip. *Note: If this strip is not wide enough to completely cover the back shoulder yoke, add a plaid scrap strip to each end as needed.*

**Step 7.** Cut two strips plaid 2" x 28 1/2" (or the length of your yoke piece); sew a strip to opposite long sides of the pieced block strip. Press seams toward strips. Remove paper from back of blocks.

**Step 8.** Center the paper yoke pattern on the pieced strip and cut out as shown in Figure 4.

**Figure 4**
Center the paper yoke pattern on the pieced strip and cut out as shown.

**Step 9.** Pin the pieced strip to the shirt's yoke back; turn under edges 1/4" all around and hand-appliqué in place.

**Step 10.** Remove buttons from pockets. Cut a 3"-wide strip plaid scrap; sew to one side of a remaining pieced block. Press seam toward strip; trim strip even with block as shown in Figure 5. Sew the strip to the opposite side, press and trim. Repeat on remaining two sides with a different 3"-wide plaid scrap strip, to frame the block as shown in Figure 6.

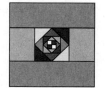

**Figure 5**
Press seam toward strip; trim strip even with block.

**Figure 6**
Repeat on remaining 2 sides to frame the block as shown.

**Step 11.** Center paper pocket pattern on the pieced unit; cut out. Remove paper from back of block. Pin the pieced pocket to the shirt pocket. Turn under 1/4" seam allowance and hand-appliqué in place. Sew button back onto shirt pocket. Repeat for second pocket.

**Step 12.** Cut three 1" x 8" bias strips from three different plaid scraps. Join the strips on the short ends to make one long strip. Fold the strip in half along length with right sides

together. Lay a 30" length of yarn or string inside along the fold, allowing 6" to dangle out one end. Pin the edges.

**Step 13.** Stitch across the opposite end and down the long open side using a scant 1/4" seam as shown in Figure 7.

**Figure 7**
Stitch across the opposite end and down the long open side using a scant 1/4" seam as shown.

**Step 14.** Trim raw edge slightly; pull the string through to turn the tube right side out. Press carefully with seam turned slightly to the backside.

**Step 15.** Pin the strip along the edge of the collar, ending at the two collar points, circling the ends and tucking the raw edges under the strip after trimming to proper length as shown in Figure 8. Hand-appliqué to shirt collar to finish. ❧

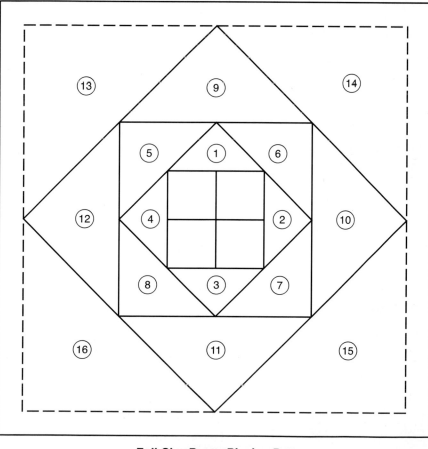

**Full-Size Paper-Piecing Pattern**
Make 7 copies

**Figure 8**
Pin the strip along the edge of the collar, ending at the 2 collar points, circling the ends and tucking the raw edges under the strip after trimming to proper length as shown.

# Around the Block

By Kathy Brown

*Covered buttons and simple patchwork blocks dress up this blue denim shirt.*

## Project Specifications

**Skill Level:** Beginner
**Shirt Size:** Size varies
**Block Size:** 3 1/4", 4 1/4", 5 1/4" or 6 1/4"
**Number of Blocks:** 7

## Materials

- 1/4 yard each blue and gold prints
- Denim shirt with pocket
- All-purpose thread to match fabrics
- 5 (3/4") ready-to-cover buttons
- 1 1/4 yards fabric stabilizer
- Basic sewing supplies and tools

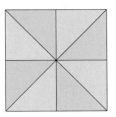

**Pinwheel**
Size of Block Varies

**Around the Block**
Placement Diagram
Size Varies

Because the size of your denim shirt may vary from small to large, the size block used will change. Measure your shirt along the bottom edge of each front side and divide this length by three. Use the block size that most closely matches your measurement. Cut fabric squares in the size listed in Step 1—the smallest square yields the smallest block size; the largest yields the largest block size.

## Instructions

**Step 1.** Cut 14 squares each gold and blue prints 2 1/2", 3", 3 1/2" or 4" based on the size block chosen for your shirt. Cut each square on one diagonal to make triangles.

**Step 2.** Sew a gold print triangle to a blue print triangle along the diagonal to make a square unit; repeat for 28 units.

**Step 3.** Join four units to complete one block as shown in Figure 1; repeat for seven blocks.

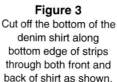

**Figure 1**
Join 4 units to complete 1 block.

**Step 4.** Join three blocks to make a strip; repeat for two strips. Press seams in one direction.

**Step 5.** Lay the shirt on a flat surface, buttoned up. Position one strip right side down on the left side of the shirt, with the right edge of the strip lining up with the edge of the button placket and positioned below the second-to-last button on the shirt as shown in Figure 2; pin in place.

**Figure 2**
Position 1 strip right side down on the left side of the shirt, with the right edge of the strip lining up with the edge of the button placket and positioned below the second-to-last button on the shirt as shown.

**Step 6.** Unbutton the bottom buttons on the shirt; position the second strip on the right side of the shirt as in Step 5, aligning this strip with the previous strip on opposite side of shirt; pin in place.

**Step 7.** Stitch along pinned edges of both strips. Remove pins, flip strips down to make right side up and press. Pin along the bottom edge and sides of each strip to hold in place; do not catch shirt back in pinning.

**Step 8.** Cut off the bottom of the denim shirt along bottom edge of strips through both front and back of shirt as shown in Figure 3.

**Step 9.** Pin fabric stabilizer around outside edges of shirt/blocks as shown in Figure 4.

**Step 10.** Using a machine satin stitch and blue thread, sew along raw edges of strip at edges of shirt as shown in Figure 5. When stitching is complete, remove fabric stabilizer.

**Figure 4**
Pin fabric stabilizer around outside edges of shirt/blocks.

**Figure 3**
Cut off the bottom of the denim shirt along bottom edge of strips through both front and back of shirt as shown.

**Figure 5**
Sew along raw edges of strip at edges of shirt as shown.

**Step 11.** Hem along bottom edge of shirt back.

**Step 12.** Pin the remaining block to the center of the shirt pocket. Satin-stitch to pocket using blue thread. ***Note:*** *If you want to use the pocket, you may turn under a seam on the block and hand-stitch in place or remove pocket from shirt before stitching in place; re-stitch the pocket to the shirt after block is stitched.*

**Step 13.** Cover the buttons using gold and blue print fabrics; replace shirt buttons with covered buttons to complete the shirt. ❥

# Home Is Where the Heart Is

By Kathy Brown

*Make this mini-purse using one flannel Log Cabin block.*

## Project Specifications

**Skill Level:** Beginner
**Purse Size:** 9 1/2" x 10"
**Block Size:** 10" x 10"
**Number of Blocks:** 1

## Materials

- 4 strips print or plaid flannel 1 1/2" x 22" for color A
- 4 strips print or plaid flannel 1 1/2" x 22" for color B
- 2 1/2" x 2 1/2" square coordinating flannel for C
- 2 1/2" x 2 1/2" square contrasting flannel for heart
- 12" x 24" flannel lining
- Backing 10 1/2" x 10 1/2"
- Neutral color all-purpose thread
- 2 1/2" x 2 1/2" square fusible transfer web
- Basic sewing supplies and tools

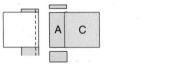

**Home Is Where the Heart Is**
Placement Diagram
9 1/2" x 10"

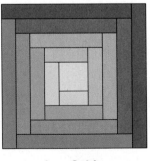

**Log Cabin**
10" x 10" Block

## Instructions

**Step 1.** Sew the C square to one of the A fabric strips; press with seam toward the A strip as shown in Figure 1. Trim strip even with center square.

**Step 2.** Place stitched unit on the same fabric strip as shown in Figure 2; stitch, press and trim as in Step 1.

**Figure 1**
Sew the center square to 1 of the A fabric strips; press with seam toward the A strip and trim as shown.

**Figure 2**
Place stitched unit on the same fabric strip.

**Step 3.** Repeat with a B fabric strip on the next two adjacent sides, stitching, pressing and trimming. Continue adding A and B strips until there are four strips on each side of the center square referring to Figure 3.

*Quick-to-Stitch Weekend Quilts & Projects*

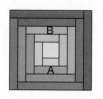

**Figure 3**
Continue adding A and
B strips until there are
4 strips on each side of
the center square.

**Step 4.** Prepare a template using heart template given. Bond the square of fusible transfer web to the wrong side of the 2 1/2" x 2 1/2" square contrasting flannel. Trace the heart shape on the paper side of the fused square. Cut out heart shape on traced line; remove paper backing.

**Step 5.** Fuse the heart shape over the center square to complete the purse front. ***Note:*** *The heart tip will be in an A strip.*

**Step 6.** Sew backing piece right sides together with block along bottom edge; press seam open and lay out flat with right side up. Place the 12" x 24" lining piece right sides together on top of the stitched unit; trim lining even with pieced unit. Sew all around, leaving a 4" opening on one side. Turn right side out through opening; hand-stitch opening closed.

**Step 7.** Fold stitched piece with right sides

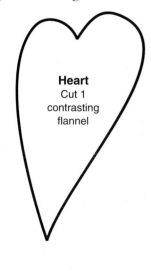

**Heart**
Cut 1
contrasting
flannel

together ***Note:*** *The right side would be the one with the pieced block.* Stitch along side seams through all layers, securing at ends.

**Step 8.** Cut a variety of flannel strips 4"–6" long and 2 1/2" wide. Join strips with right sides together on short ends to make a strip approximately 46" long for strap; press seams open.

**Step 9.** Fold the strip with right sides together; stitch along length. Turn right side out through ends; press with seam on side.

**Step 10.** Slip ends of strap inside bag at side seams as shown in Figure 4; stitch in place securely to finish. ❧

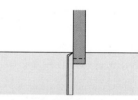

**Figure 4**
Slip ends of strap inside bag at side
seams; stitch to secure.

# Frosty Stars Lap Quilt

By Holly Daniels

*The crisp blue-and-white color scheme of this cozy lap quilt is perfect for the winter season. Try using fabrics with swirling prints to create the snowy theme.*

## Project Specifications

**Skill Level:** Intermediate
**Project Size:** 52" x 52"
**Block Size:** 12" x 12"
**Number of Blocks:** 9

## Materials

- 1/2 yard each light and dark blue prints
- 5/8 yard red print
- 3/4 yard snowflake print
- 1 yard white-on-white print
- Backing 56" x 56"
- Batting 56" x 56"
- 6 1/4 yards self-made or purchased binding
- Neutral color all-purpose thread
- Basic sewing supplies and tools

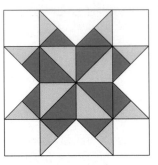

**Frosty Stars**
12" x 12" Block

## Instructions

**Step 1.** Cut three strips white-on-white print 3 1/2" by fabric width; subcut into 3 1/2" square segments for A. You will need 36 A squares. Cut one strip white-on-white print 2 1/2" by fabric width; subcut into 2 1/2" square segments for B sashing squares. You will need 16 B squares.

**Step 2.** Cut two strips white-on-white print 7 1/4" by fabric width; subcut into nine 7 1/4" squares. Cut each square in half on both diagonals to make 36 C triangles.

**Step 3.** Cut two strips each light and dark blue prints 4 1/4" by fabric width; subcut into eighteen 4 1/4" squares each color. Cut each square in half on both diagonals to make 72 D triangles of each color.

**Step 4.** Sew a light blue print D to a dark blue print D as shown in Figure 1; repeat for 36 D1 units. Turn pieces and join remaining pieces to make 36 D2 units, again referring to Figure 1.

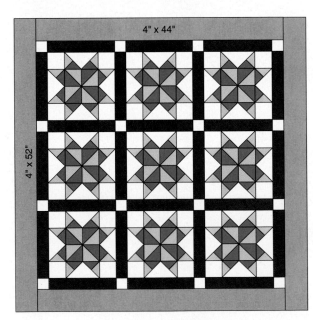

**Frosty Stars Lap Quilt**
Placement Diagram
52" x 52"

4" x 44"

4" x 52"

**D1 Unit**   **D2 Unit**
Make 36      Make 36

**Figure 1**
Join D triangles as
shown to make D units.

**Step 5.** Sew a D1 and D2 unit to the short sides of C as shown in Figure 2; repeat for 36 C-D units and set aside.

**Figure 2**
Sew a D1 and D2 unit to the
short sides of C as shown.

**Step 6.** Cut two strips each light and dark blue prints 3 7/8" by fabric width; subcut strips into 3 7/8" square segments. Cut each square in half on one diagonal to make E triangles; you will need 36 E triangles of each color.

**Step 7.** Sew light and dark blue print E triangles together as shown in Figure 3; repeat for all E triangles to make 36 E units.

**Step 8.** Join four E units as shown in Figure 4 to complete one block center; repeat for nine block centers.

**Figure 3**
Sew light and dark
blue print E triangles
together as shown.

**Figure 4**
Join 4 E units as
shown to complete
1 block center.

**Step 9.** To complete one block, sew a C-D unit to two opposite sides of a block center. Sew an A square on each end of two C-D units; sew an A-C-D unit to two opposite sides of the pieced center unit to complete one block as shown in Figure 5.

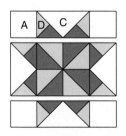

**Figure 5**
Sew an A-C-D unit to 2
opposite sides of the pieced
center unit to complete 1 block.

**Step 10.** Repeat Step 9 to complete nine blocks.

**Step 11.** Cut eight strips red print 2 1/2" by fabric width; subcut into 12 1/2" segments for sashing strips. You will need 24 sashing strips.

**Step 12.** Join four B sashing squares with three sashing strips to make a sashing row as shown in Figure 6; repeat for four sashing rows. Press seams toward B.

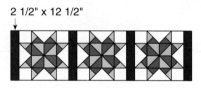

**Figure 6**
Join 4 B sashing squares with 3
sashing strips to make a sashing row.

**Step 13.** Join three blocks with four sashing strips to make a block row as shown in Figure 7; repeat for three block rows. Press seams toward sashing strips.

**Figure 7**
Join 3 blocks with 4 sashing
strips to make a block row.

**Step 14.** Join the block rows and the sashing rows to complete the pieced center referring to the Placement Diagram; press seams in one direction.

**Step 15.** Cut and piece two strips each snowflake print 4 1/2" x 44 1/2" and 4 1/2" x 52 1/2". Sew the shorter strips to the top and bottom and longer strips to opposite sides to complete the pieced top; press seams toward strips.

**Step 16.** Prepare top for quilting, quilt and bind referring to the General Instructions. ***Note:*** *The quilt shown was machine-quilted in a meandering design.* ❧

# The Sun, the Moon & the Stars

By Jill Reber

*This peaceful-looking wall banner is the perfect bedroom accent.*

## Project Specifications

**Skill Level:** Intermediate
**Project Size:** 28" x 48"
**Block Size:** 4" x 4" and 20" x 20"
**Number of Blocks:** 10 small, 1 large

## Materials

- Scraps yellow prints for star appliqués
- 2 1/2" by fabric width strips 5 different yellow prints
- 1/4 yard each gold and light blue prints
- 1/4 yard orange mottled
- 14 5/8" x 14 5/8" square medium blue print
- 5/8 yard dark blue print
- 5/8 yard white solid
- Backing 32" x 52"
- Batting 32" x 52"
- 4 3/4 yards self-made or purchased binding
- All-purpose thread to match fabrics
- Variegated yellow rayon thread
- 3/8 yard fusible transfer web
- 1/2 yard tear-off fabric stabilizer
- Blue 6-strand embroidery floss
- Basic sewing supplies and tools, water-erasable marker or pencil

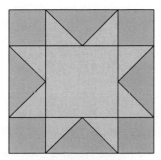

**Evening Star**
4" x 4" Block

## Instructions

**Step 1.** Cut 12 squares white solid and 16 squares gold print 2 7/8" x 2 7/8". Cut each square on one diagonal to make A triangles.

**Step 2.** Sew a gold print A triangle to a white solid A triangle as shown in Figure 1; repeat for 24 A units. Set aside remaining A triangles.

**Figure 1**
Sew a gold print A triangle to a white solid A triangle as shown.

**Step 3.** Cut two squares orange mottled 6 7/8" x 6 7/8"; cut each square on one diagonal to make four B triangles.

**Step 4.** Cut four squares white solid 2 1/2" x 2 1/2" for C.

**Step 5.** Join three A units to make a strip as shown in Figure 2; repeat for eight strips. Sew a C square to the gold print end of four strips as shown in Figure 3.

Make 4

Make 4

**Figure 2**
Join 3 A units to make a strip.

**Figure 3**
Sew a C square to the gold print end of 4 strips.

**Step 6.** Sew a remaining gold print A triangle to the end of each strip referring to Figure 4. Join the pieced units with B to make a large triangle unit as shown in Figure 5; repeat for four large triangle units.

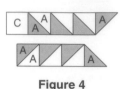
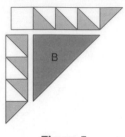

**Figure 4**
Sew a remaining gold print A triangle to the end of each strip.

**Figure 5**
Join the pieced units with B to make a large triangle unit.

**Step 7.** Sew a large triangle unit to each side of the 14 5/8" x 14 5/8" square medium blue print to complete one Rising Sun Variation block as shown in Figure 6; set aside.

sides of an E square. Sew D to each end of the remaining two F-G units; repeat for two D-F-G units. Sew a D-F-G unit to opposite sides of the E-F-G unit to complete one Evening Star block as shown in Figure 8; repeat for 10 blocks, two from each yellow print.

**Figure 7**
Sew an F triangle to each short side of G to make an F-G unit as shown.

**Figure 8**
Join units to complete 1 Evening Star block.

**Figure 6**
Sew a large triangle unit to each side of the medium blue print square to complete 1 Rising Sun Variation block.

**Step 8.** To make Evening Star blocks, cut two strips light blue print 1 1/2" by fabric width; subcut into 1 1/2" square segments for D; you will need 40 D squares.

**Step 9.** Cut two 2 1/2" x 2 1/2" squares from each yellow print strip for E; you will need 10 E squares.

**Step 10.** Cut eight 1 7/8" x 1 7/8" squares from each yellow print strip; cut each square on one diagonal to make F triangles. You will need a total of 80 F triangles.

**Step 11.** Cut 10 squares light blue print 3 1/4" x 3 1/4"; cut each square on both diagonals to make G triangles; you will need 40 G triangles.

**Step 12.** Sort yellow triangles and squares together in piles of like fabrics. To make one Evening Star block, sew an F triangle to each short side of G to make an F-G unit as shown in Figure 7; repeat for four units.

**Step 13.** Sew an F-G unit to two opposite

**The Sun, the Moon & the Stars**
Placement Diagram
28" x 48"

**Step 14.** Join five Evening Star blocks to make a row; press seams in one direction. Repeat for two rows.

**Step 15.** Cut two strips each white solid 2 1/2" x 20 1/2" and 4 1/2" x 20 1/2".

**Step 16.** Sew an Evening Star block strip between one 2 1/2"-wide and one 4 1/2"-wide white solid strip; press seams toward white solid strips.

**Step 17.** Sew the strip sections to the Rising Sun Variation center block; press seams away from center block.

**Step 18.** Transfer the messages to the wider white solid strips using patterns given and water-erasable marker or pencil and referring to the Placement Diagram for positioning.

**Step 19.** Stem-stitch letters using 2 strands blue embroidery floss. Make three French knots at the end of the message.

**Step 20.** Prepare templates for moon and star shapes using patterns given. Trace shapes onto the paper side of the fusible transfer web referring to patterns for number to cut; cut out shapes leaving a margin around each one.

**Step 21.** Fuse shapes to the wrong side of fabrics as directed on pattern pieces for color. Cut out

shapes on traced line; remove paper backing.

**Step 22.** Arrange moon and one star of each size on the medium blue print center square referring to the Placement Diagram for positioning; fuse shapes in place. Arrange two medium and one small star on the bottom wide white solid strip after the message, again referring to the Placement Diagram for positioning; fuse shapes in place.

**Step 23.** Pin a piece of tear-off fabric stabilizer behind shapes. Machine satin-stitch around each fused shape using variegated yellow rayon thread; remove tear-off fabric stabilizer when appliqué is complete.

**Step 24.** Cut (and piece if necessary) two strips each 4 1/2" x 20 1/2" and 4 1/2" x 48 1/2" dark blue print. Sew shorter strips to the top and bottom and longer strips to opposite sides of the pieced center; press seams toward strips.

**Step 25.** Prepare for quilting, quilt and bind referring to the General Instructions. ***Note:*** *The quilt shown was machine-quilted in a meandering design and through the star points as shown in Figure 9 using all-purpose thread to match fabrics.* ❧

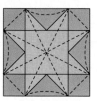

**Figure 9**
Evening Star blocks
were quilted as shown.

**Medium Star**
Cut 3 yellow print

**Small Star**
Cut 2 yellow print

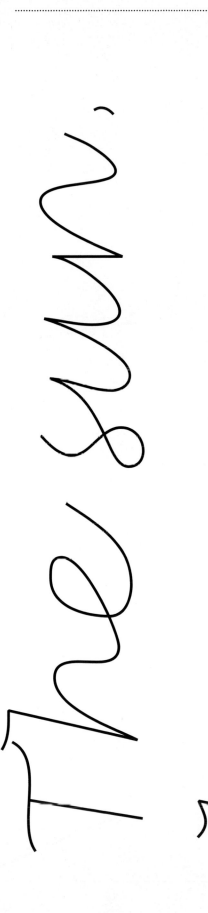

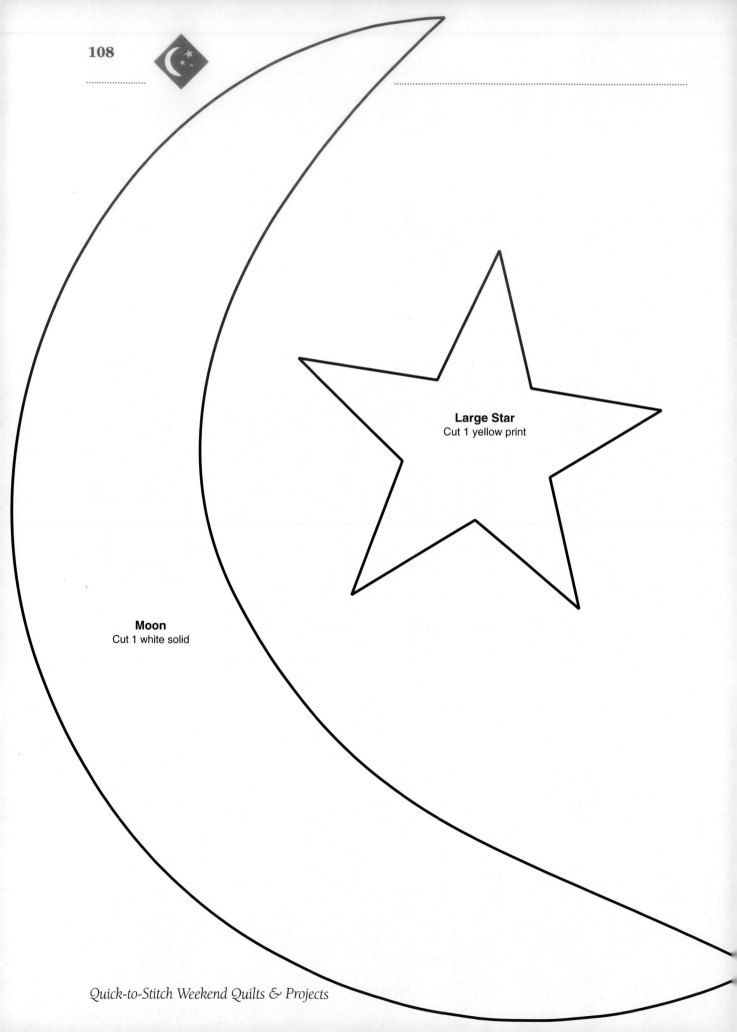

**Large Star**
Cut 1 yellow print

**Moon**
Cut 1 white solid

# Forever Patriotic

By Jill Reber

*Change your decorative look with the seasons with a matching wall quilt and pillow covers.*

## Project Specifications

**Skill Level:** Intermediate

**Wall Quilt Size:** 46" x 46"

**Pillow Cover Size:** 20" x 20"

**Block Size:** 16" x 16"

**Number of Blocks:** 8

## Materials

- 1/4 yard navy-and-burgundy stripe
- 3/8 yard tan mottled
- 1/2 yard tan check
- 3/4 yard burgundy-and-cream stripe
- 1 yard total burgundy tone-on-tone prints
- 1 1/4 yards total blue tone-on-tone prints
- 1 1/4 yards total cream-on-cream prints
- 2 1/2 yards muslin
- Backing 50" x 50" for wall quilt
- 4 squares backing 21" x 21" for pillows
- Batting 50" x 50"
- 5 1/2 yards self-made or purchased binding
- Neutral color all-purpose thread
- 4 (20") burgundy nylon zippers
- 4 (20") pillow forms
- Basic sewing supplies and tools

**Flag**
16" x 16" Block

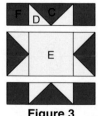

**Flag Pillow**
Placement Diagram
20" x 20"

# Instructions

## Flag Block

**Step 1.** Cut three strips each cream-on-cream and burgundy tone-on-tone prints 2 1/2" by fabric width; subcut into four 16 1/2" segments for A and four 8 1/2" segments for B from each color.

**Step 2.** Cut two squares blue-on-blue print 5 1/4" x 5 1/4"; cut on both diagonals to make eight C triangles.

**Step 3.** Cut eight squares cream-on-cream print 2 7/8" x 2 7/8"; cut each square on one diagonal to make 16 D triangles.

**Step 4.** Cut two squares 4 1/2" x 4 1/2" cream-on-cream print for E.

**Step 5.** Cut eight squares blue-on-blue print 2 1/2" x 2 1/2" for F.

**Step 6.** Sew a D triangle to each short side of C referring to Figure 1; repeat for four units.

**Step 7.** Sew a C-D unit to opposite sides of E referring to Figure 2.

**Step 8.** Sew an F square to each end of the remaining C-D units. Sew a C-D-F unit to the long sides of the C-D-E unit to complete one star unit as shown in Figure 3.

4" x 4"

4" x 38"

**Forever Patriotic Quilt**
Placement Diagram
46" x 46"

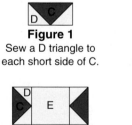

**Figure 1**
Sew a D triangle to each short side of C.

**Figure 2**
Sew a C-D unit to opposite sides of E.

**Figure 3**
Sew a C-D-F unit to the long sides of the C-D-E unit to complete 1 star unit.

**Step 9.** Join the A strips as shown in Figure 4; repeat for B strips, again referring to Figure 4.

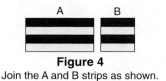

**Figure 4**
Join the A and B strips as shown.

**Step 10.** Sew the star unit to the B unit as shown in Figure 5; join with the A unit to complete one Flag block as shown in Figure 6. Repeat for two blocks; set aside.

**Figure 5**
Sew the star unit to the B unit as shown.

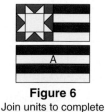

**Figure 6**
Join units to complete 1 Flag block.

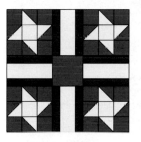

**Rolling Stars**
16" x 16" Block

**Rolling Stars Pillow**
Placement Diagram
20" x 20"

### Rolling Stars Block

**Step 1.** Cut two strips blue-on-blue print 2 1/2" by fabric width; subcut into 2 1/2" square segments for 32 F squares. Cut eight 2 1/2" x 2 1/2" squares cream-on-cream print for F.

**Step 2.** Cut two strips each cream-on-cream and blue tone-on-tone prints 2 7/8" by fabric width; subcut strips into 2 7/8" square segments. Cut each segment in half to make 32 D triangles of each color.

**Step 3.** Sew a cream-on-cream print D to a blue tone-on-tone print D as shown in Figure 7; repeat to make 32 D units.

**Figure 7**
Sew a cream-on-cream print D to a blue tone-on-tone print D.

**Step 4.** Arrange four D units in rows with four dark and one light F square referring to Figure 8. Join in rows; join the rows to complete one

**Figure 8**
Arrange 4 D units in rows with 4 dark and 1 light F square to complete 1 rolling star unit.

rolling star unit. Repeat for eight units.

**Step 5.** Cut four strips burgundy tone-on-tone print 1 1/2" by fabric width and two strips cream-on-cream print 2 1/2" by fabric width. Sew a light strip between two dark strips along length with right sides together; press seams toward dark strips. Repeat for two strip sets. Subcut strip sets into eight 6 1/2" segments for G.

**Step 6.** Cut two squares blue tone-on-tone print 4 1/2" x 4 1/2" for H.

**Step 7.** Arrange the rolling star units with the G units and the H square in rows referring to Figure 9. Join the units in rows; join the rows to complete one Rolling Stars block. Repeat for two blocks; set aside.

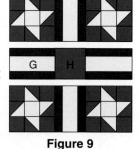

**Figure 9**
Arrange the rolling star units with the G units and the H square in rows to complete 1 Rolling Stars block.

**Flag Stars**
16" x 16" Block

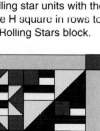

**Flag Stars Pillow**
Placement Diagram
20" x 20"

### Flag Stars Block

**Step 1.** Cut two strips each burgundy tone-on-tone and cream-on-cream prints 1 1/2" by fabric width. Sew a light strip to a dark strip with right sides together along length; press seams toward dark strip. Repeat for two strip sets.

**Step 2.** Subcut strip sets into twelve 2 1/2" segments for I and twelve 4 1/2" segments for J.

**Step 3.** Cut two strips blue tone-on-tone print 2 1/2" by fabric width; subcut into 2 1/2" square segments for F. You will need 28 F squares.

**Step 4.** Sew an F square to an I segment as shown in Figure 10; repeat for 12 units. Sew a J segment to each F-I unit to complete a small flag unit as shown in Figure 11; repeat for 12 units and set aside.

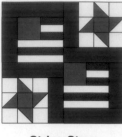

**Figure 10**
Sew an F square
to an I segment.

**Figure 11**
Sew a J segment to each F-I unit
to complete a small flag unit.

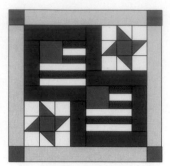

**Stripe Stars**
16" x 16" Block

**Stripe Stars Pillow**
Placement Diagram
20" x 20"

**Step 5.** Cut four squares blue tone-on-tone print 5 1/4" x 5 1/4"; cut each square on both diagonals to make 16 C triangles.

**Step 6.** Cut two strips tan mottled 2 7/8" by fabric width; subcut into 2 7/8" square segments. You will need 16 squares; cut each square in half on one diagonal to make 32 D triangles.

**Step 7.** Sew a D triangle to each short side of C as shown in Figure 1; repeat for 16 C-D units.

**Step 8.** Cut four squares each tan mottled and burgundy tone-on-tone print 4 7/8" x 4 7/8". Cut each square in half on one diagonal to make eight K triangles from each color. Sew a light K to a dark K to make a K unit as shown in Figure 12; repeat for eight K units.

**Step 9.** Piece one flag/star unit referring to Figure 13; repeat for four flag/star units.

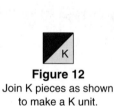

**Figure 12**
Join K pieces as shown
to make a K unit.

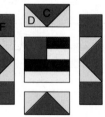

**Figure 13**
Join pieces to make 1
flag/star unit as shown.

**Step 10.** Piece one flag/K unit referring to Figure 14; repeat for four flag/K units.

**Step 11.** Join two flag/star units and two flag/K units to complete one Flag Stars block referring to Figure 15.

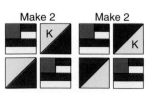

Make 2          Make 2

**Figure 14**
Join pieces to make
flag/K units as shown.

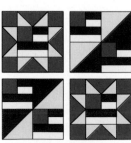

**Figure 15**
Join units to complete 1
Flag Stars block as shown.

## Stripe Stars Block

**Step 1.** Cut three strips burgundy tone-on-tone print and three strips cream-on-cream print 1 1/2" by fabric width. Sew a dark strip between two light strips with right sides together along length; press seams toward dark strip. Subcut strip set into four 6 1/2" segments for L.

**Step 2.** Sew a light strip between two dark strips with right sides together along length; press seams toward dark strips. Subcut strip set into four 3 1/2" segments for M.

**Step 3.** Cut four squares blue tone-on-tone print 3 1/2" x 3 1/2" for N.

**Step 4.** Sew an N square to an M unit as shown in Figure 16; repeat for four units. Sew an L unit to each M-N unit to make flag units, again referring to Figure 16.

**Figure 16**
Sew N to M; add L to
complete 1 flag unit.

**Step 5.** Cut three strips navy-and-burgundy stripe 2 1/2" by fabric width; subcut into eight 6 1/2" segments for O and eight 8 1/2" segments for P.

**Step 6.** Sew O and P to a flag unit as shown in Figure 17; repeat for four units. Set aside.

**Figure 17**
Sew O and P
to a flag unit.

**Step 7.** Cut one strip cream-on-cream print 2 1/2" by fabric width; subcut into 2 1/2" square segments for 16 F squares. Cut four 2 1/2" x 2 1/2" squares blue tone-on-tone print for F.

**Step 8.** Cut one strip each cream-on-cream and blue tone-on-tone prints 2 7/8" by fabric width; subcut strips into 2 7/8" square segments. Cut each segment in half to make 16 D triangles of each color.

**Step 9.** Sew a cream-on-cream print D to a blue tone-on-tone print D referring to Figure 7; repeat to make 16 D units.

**Step 10.** Arrange four D units in rows with one dark and four light F squares referring to Figure 18. Join in rows; join the rows to complete one rolling star unit. Repeat for four units.

**Step 11.** Sew O and P to a rolling star unit as shown in Figure 19; repeat to make four units.

**Figure 18**
Arrange 4 D units in rows with 1 dark and 4 light F squares.

**Figure 19**
Sew O and P to a rolling star unit as shown.

**Step 12.** Join two each rolling stars and flag units to complete one Stripe Stars block referring to Figure 20; repeat for two blocks.

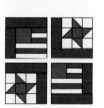

**Figure 20**
Join 2 flag units with 2 rolling star units to complete 1 Stripe Stars block.

## Making Quilt

**Step 1.** Cut one strip tan check 16 1/2" by fabric width; subcut strip into 2 1/2" segments to make sashing strips. You will need 12 sashing strips.

**Step 2.** Cut nine 2 1/2" x 2 1/2" squares blue tone-on-tone print for sashing squares.

**Step 3.** Choose one of each of the previously pieced blocks. Join two blocks with three sashing strips to make a block row referring to the Placement Diagram for positioning of blocks; repeat for two block rows. Press seams toward strips.

**Step 4.** Join two sashing strips with three sashing squares to make a sashing row as shown in Figure 21; repeat for three sashing rows. Press seams toward sashing strips.

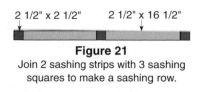

2 1/2" x 2 1/2"     2 1/2" x 16 1/2"

**Figure 21**
Join 2 sashing strips with 3 sashing squares to make a sashing row.

**Step 5.** Join the block rows and the sashing rows to complete the pieced center; press seams in one direction.

**Step 6.** Cut four strips burgundy-and-cream stripe 4 1/2" x 38 1/2" for borders. Sew a strip to two opposite sides of the pieced center; press seams toward strips.

**Step 7.** Cut four squares blue tone-on-tone print 4 1/2" x 4 1/2"; sew a square to each end of the remaining two border strips. Sew these strips to the remaining sides to complete the pieced top.

**Step 8.** Prepare top for quilting, quilt and bind referring to the General Instructions. ***Note:*** *The quilt shown was machine-quilted in a meandering design. Star designs were hand-quilted in some of the blue tone-on-tone print squares using white quilting thread. Use the star patterns given for appliqué for The Sun, the Moon & the Stars quilt on page 106.*

## Making Pillow

**Step 1.** Cut four strips burgundy-and-cream stripe 2 1/2" x 16 1/2" for borders and four squares blue tone-on-tone print 2 1/2" x 2 1/2".

**Step 2.** Sew a border strip to two opposite sides of one of the pieced blocks; press seams toward strips. Sew a square to each end of the remaining two strips; sew a strip to the remaining sides of the block to complete the pieced pillow top referring to the Placement Diagrams for the pillows.

**Step 3.** Cut two pieces of muslin using the pillow top as a pattern. Layer one muslin square wrong sides together with a backing square and finish all edges using a serger or a machine zigzag stitch. Repeat with pillow top and second muslin square.

**Step 4.** Using your favorite zipper insertion method, or following the directions with the zipper, insert the zipper on the bottom edge of the pillow front and back.

**Step 5.** Unzip the zipper; place pillow front and back right sides together. Stitch all around sides; turn right side out through zipper opening.

**Step 6.** Insert pillow form and zip opening closed to finish. Repeat for four pillow tops using previously pieced blocks. ❧

# Blessed Are the Piecemakers

By Janice Loewenthal

*The piecemakers referred to in this quilted message are those who stitch pieces together, not those who make peace.*

## Project Specifications

**Skill Level:** Intermediate
**Project Size:** 24" x 24"
**Block Size:** 8" x 8"
**Number of Blocks:** 8

## Materials

- 1 fat quarter each burgundy, blue, gold and green prints or solids
- 1 fat quarter each tan and cream checks, tan dot, burgundy print and yellow mottled
- 8 1/2" x 8 1/2" square gold mottled
- Backing 28" x 28"
- Batting 28" x 28"
- 3 1/4 yards self-made or purchased binding
- Cream, blue and black all-purpose thread
- Clear nylon monofilament
- 1/4 yard fusible transfer web
- 1/4 yard tear-off fabric stabilizer
- Black 6-strand embroidery floss
- Basic sewing supplies and tools, water-erasable marker or pencil

## Instructions

**Step 1.** To make Spool blocks, cut two strips each from the fat quarters of burgundy, blue, gold and green prints or solids 1" x 21". Sew one strip of each color with right sides together along length in any order or the order shown in Figure 1; press seams in one direction. Repeat for two strip sets.

**Step 2.** Cut each strip set into 4 1/2" segments for spool center units as shown in Figure 1. You will need eight segments.

**Step 3.** Join two segments as shown in Figure 2 to complete one D unit; repeat for four D units.

**Framed 16-Patch**
8" x 8" Block
Make 2

**Stars & Heart**
8" x 8" Block
Make 2

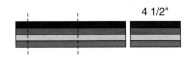

**Spool**
8" x 8" Block
Make 4

**Step 4.** Cut eight squares each tan dot and tan check 2 7/8" x 2 7/8". Cut each square on one diagonal to make tan check B and tan dot C triangles. You will need 16 each B and C triangles.

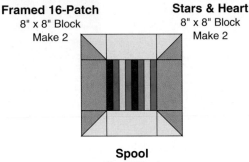

**Figure 1**
Cut each strip set into 4 1/2" segments
for spool center unit as shown.

**Figure 2**
Join 2 segments to
complete 1 D unit.

**Step 5.** Cut two strips each tan check and tan dot 2 1/2" x 21"; subcut into 4 1/2" segments for tan print A and tan check E. You will need eight each A and E rectangles.

**Step 6.** To piece one Spool block, sew B to C

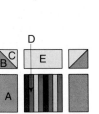

**Figure 3**
Arrange the B-C units with
A, D and E in rows.

along diagonal edge to make a square; repeat for four units. Arrange the B-C units with A, D and E in rows referring to Figure 3. Join units in rows; join rows to complete one Spool block. Repeat for four Spool blocks; set aside.

**Step 7.** For the Framed 16-Patch blocks, cut one strip each from the fat quarters of burgundy, blue, gold and green prints or solids 1 1/2" x 21". Join strips with right sides together along length to make a strip set in the color order shown in Figure 4.

**Step 8.** Cut each strip set into 1 1/2" segments as shown in Figure 4.

**Step 9.** Join segments as shown in Figure 5 to make a 16-patch H center unit; repeat for two units referring to the Placement Diagram for positioning segments.

**Figure 4**
Cut strip set into
1 1/2" segments
as shown.

**Figure 5**
Join segments
as shown to
make a 16-patch
H center unit.

**Step 10.** Cut two strips burgundy print 2 1/2" x 21"; subcut strips into 4 1/2" segments for F. You will need eight F pieces.

**Step 11.** Cut one strip burgundy solid 2 1/2" x 21"; subcut into 2 1/2" segments for G. You will need eight G squares.

**Step 12.** To make one Framed 16-Patch block, arrange F, G and H units in rows referring to Figure 6; join units in rows. Join rows to

*Quick Classics*

**Blessed Are the Piecemakers**
Placement Diagram
24" x 24"

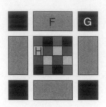

**Figure 6**
Join F, G and H units as
shown to make a Framed
16-Patch block.

complete one Framed 16-Patch block;
repeat for two blocks and set aside.

**Step 13.** Cut two cream check rectangles
5 1/2" x 8 1/2" for I and two each burgundy and green solid or print rectangles
3 1/2" x 4 1/2" for J. Join the pieces as
shown in Figure 7 to make Stars & Heart
base block; repeat for two blocks.

**Figure 7**
Join pieces as shown
to make Stars &
Heart base block.

**Step 14.** Make templates for heart and
star shapes using patterns given. Trace
shapes onto the paper side of the fusible
transfer web as directed on patterns for
number to cut.

**Step 15.** Cut out shapes, leaving a margin around each one. Fuse shapes to the
wrong side of fabrics as directed on patterns; cut out shapes on traced lines.
Remove paper backing.

**Step 16.** Fuse one star shape onto each J
piece and a heart shape onto each I
piece. Fuse needle shapes onto heart
shapes referring to the Placement
Diagram for positioning of pieces.

**Step 17.** Transfer message to center
square using a water-erasable marker or
pencil. Stem-stitch letters using 3 strands
black embroidery floss.

**Step 18.** Place a piece of tear-off fabric
stabilizer behind each heart and star
shape. Machine satin-stitch around needle
shapes using blue all-purpose thread.

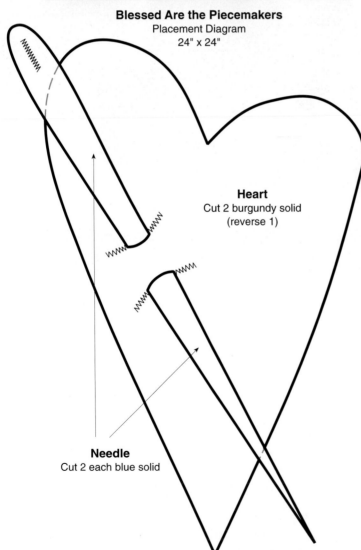

**Heart**
Cut 2 burgundy solid
(reverse 1)

**Needle**
Cut 2 each blue solid

Machine satin-stitch needle ends and eyes using black all-purpose thread. Machine buttonhole-stitch around each heart and star shape using black all-purpose thread. Draw thread lines from needle eyes and straight-stitch using black all-purpose thread; remove fabric stabilizer.

**Step 19.** Arrange pieced blocks in three rows of three blocks each with the gold mottled square; join blocks in rows. Join rows to complete the pieced center.

**Step 20.** Prepare for quilting, quilt and bind referring to the General Instructions. ***Note:*** *The quilt shown was machine-quilted 1/8" away from each heart and star shape using cream all-purpose thread and in the ditch of seams using clear nylon monofilament.* ❧

**Star**
Cut 4 yellow mottled
(reverse half)

**Message**
Transfer to 8 1/2" x 8 1/2" gold mottled square

# Circle of Leaves

By Carla Schwab

*The leaf-shaped pieces in this table mat are machine-appliquéd to avoid the challenge of curved piecing.*

## Project Specifications

**Skill Level:** Intermediate
**Project Size:** 36" x 36"
**Block Size:** 4 1/2" x 4 1/2"
**Number of Blocks:** 64

## Materials

- 3/4 yard dark green mottled
- 3/4 yard each yellow and coral prints
- 1 yard total of a variety of light green prints
- Backing 40" x 40"
- Batting 40" x 40"
- Neutral color all-purpose thread
- Green variegated rayon thread
- Green quilting thread
- Basic sewing supplies and tools

**Yellow Leaf**
4 1/2" x 4 1/2" Block
Make 32

**Coral Leaf**
4 1/2" x 4 1/2" Block
Make 32

## Instructions

**Step 1.** Cut 32 squares each yellow and coral prints 5" x 5".

**Step 2.** Prepare template for piece A using pattern given. Cut 64 A pieces from the various light green prints.

**Step 3.** Cut 11 strips dark green mottled 2" by fabric width.

**Step 4.** Sew the various light green print pieces to the dark green mottled strips, placing right sides together and sewing along the straight edge using a 1/4" seam allowance as shown in Figure 1.

**Figure 1**
Sew the various light green print pieces to the dark green mottled strips, placing right sides together and sewing along the straight edge using a 1/4" seam allowance as shown.

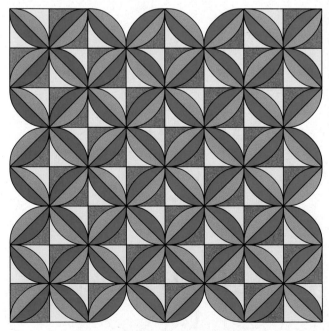

**Circle of Leaves**
Placement Diagram
36" x 36"

**Step 5.** Using the light green print half as the template, trim away the outside edge of dark green print as shown in Figure 2; press open to make a leaf shape as shown in Figure 3.

Trim

**Figure 2**
Using the light green print half as the template, trim away the outside edge of dark green print as shown.

**Figure 3**
Press open to make a leaf shape.

**Step 6.** Place a leaf shape on each yellow and coral print square as shown in Figure 4; pin in place.

**Figure 4**
Place a leaf shape on each yellow and coral print square.

**Step 7.** Using green variegated rayon thread, machine satin-stitch each leaf shape in place to complete blocks.

**Step 8.** Join four yellow and four coral blocks to make a row referring to Figure 5; repeat for four rows. Press seams in one direction.

**Figure 5**
Join 4 yellow and 4 coral blocks to make a row.

**Step 9.** Join four coral and four yellow blocks to make a row referring to Figure 6; repeat for four rows. Press seams in one direction.

**Figure 6**
Join 4 coral and 4 yellow blocks to make a row.

**Step 10.** Join the rows referring to the Placement Diagram to complete pieced top; press seams in one direction.

**Step 11.** Lay quilt top right side up on a flat surface; place prepared backing fabric right sides together with pieced top. Place batting piece on top of backing; pin layers together firmly to hold flat.

**Step 12.** Stitch around outside edges of quilt, 1/4" away from edge of pieced top, leaving a 6" opening right after the corner on one side. Trim excess batting and backing even with pieced top edge.

**Step 13.** Stitch close to the leaf edge on the center four leaf sections of one side as shown in Figure 7; repeat on all four sides. Trim away excess beyond seam as shown in Figure 8.

**Figure 7**
Stitch close to the leaf edge on the center 4 leaf sections of 1 side.

**Figure 8**
Trim away excess beyond seam as shown.

**Step 14.** Turn right side out through opening; hand-stitch opening closed.

**Step 15.** Hand- or machine-quilt close to the edges of each leaf section using green quilting thread to finish. ❧

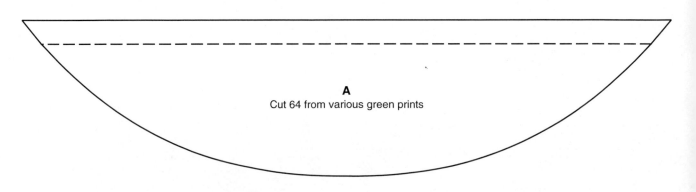

**A**
Cut 64 from various green prints

# Sunbonnet Sue

By Marian Shenk

*Make this Sunbonnet Sue pillow
using soft, warm colors to match
your favorite relaxing spot.*

## Instructions

**Step 1.** Cut two 15" x 15" squares cream-on-cream print; set one aside for pillow back. Fold and crease the remaining square to mark centers.

**Step 2.** Prepare templates for hand appliqué using patterns given and referring to the General Instructions.

**Step 3.** Center the appliqué pieces and layer in numerical order on the pillow front piece using

### Project Specifications

**Skill Level:** Intermediate
**Pillow Size:** 14" x 14" (without ruffle)

### Materials

- Scraps pink and white prints
- Scrap black solid
- 1/2 yard cream-on-cream print
- 3/4 yard blue print
- Muslin lining 15" x 15"
- Batting 15" x 15"
- All-purpose thread to match fabrics
- Off-white quilting thread
- 2 yards (3/8") pink corded piping
- 1 (5mm) white bead
- 1 (3/4") pink flower
- 1 (3") length 1/4"-wide pink satin ribbon
- 14" pillow form
- Basic sewing supplies and tools and zipper foot

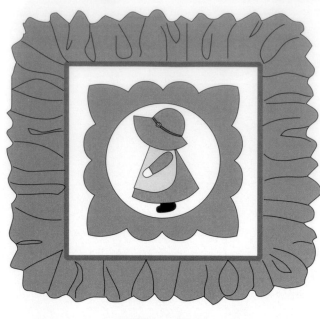

**Sunbonnet Sue**
Placement Diagram
14" x 14"
(without ruffle)

creases as guides. Hand-appliqué pieces in place in numerical order referring to the General Instructions. Repeat with blue print frame piece.

**Step 4.** Hand-stitch the 1/4"-wide pink ribbon on the hat piece, folding in ends. Sew the 3/4" pink flower on the ribbon and the 5mm white bead in place on the flower referring to the pattern and Placement Diagram for positioning.

**Step 5.** Sandwich batting square between muslin lining and appliquéd top; pin layers together to hold.

**Step 6.** Quilt as desired by hand or machine. *Note: The pillow shown was outline-quilted by hand using off-white quilting thread.* Machine-baste around outside edges.

**Step 7.** When quilting is complete, lay pink corded piping right sides together with pillow top, matching raw edges. Sew in place, using a 1/2" seam allowance and a zipper foot.

**Step 8.** Cut two strips blue print 5" by fabric width; join the strips on the short ends to make a tube. Fold in half with wrong sides together to make a double-layered tube for ruffle as shown in Figure 1.

**Figure 1**
Fold in half with wrong sides together
to make a double-layered tube for ruffle.

**Step 9.** Sew two lines of gathering stitches close to raw edge of tube. Divide the tube in quarters; mark with a pin. Match pinned areas with corners of quilted pillow top as shown in Figure 2.

**Figure 2**
Match pinned areas with
corners of quilted pillow top.

**Step 10.** Pull threads to gather ruffle to fit evenly around pillow top; stitch in place using a 1/2" seam allowance.

**Step 11.** Place the pillow back right sides together with pillow top; stitch all around, using a 1/2" seam allowance and leaving an 8" opening on one side.

**Step 12.** Insert pillow form through opening; hand-stitch opening closed to finish. ❧

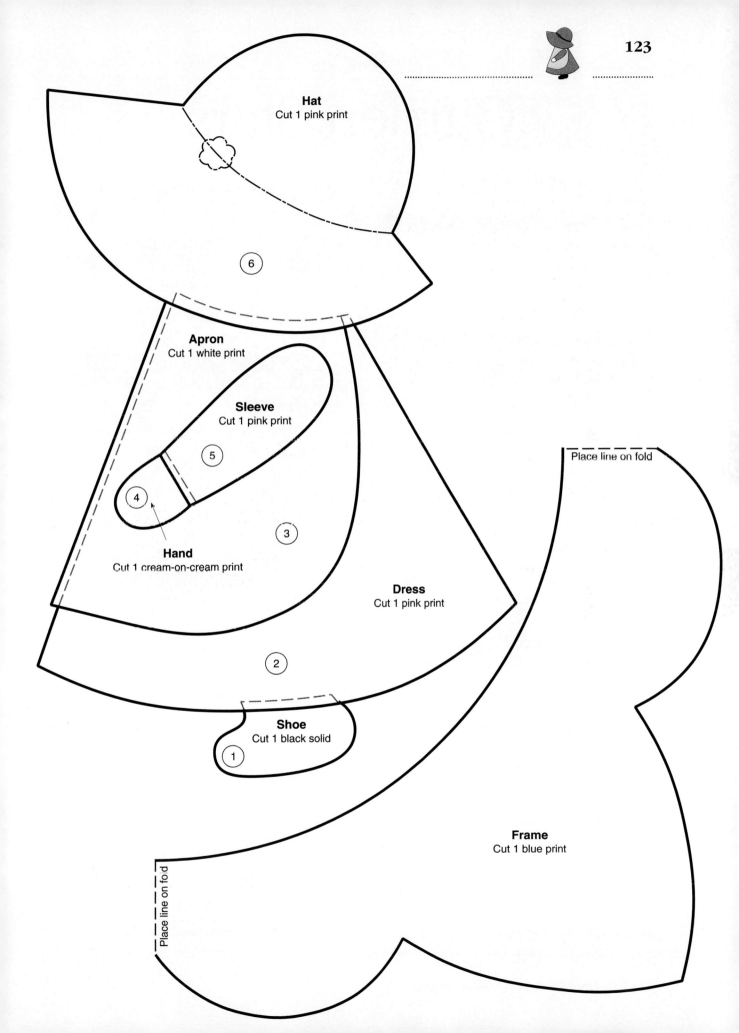

**Hat**
Cut 1 pink print

6

**Apron**
Cut 1 white print

**Sleeve**
Cut 1 pink print

5

4

**Hand**
Cut 1 cream-on-cream print

3

**Dress**
Cut 1 pink print

Place line on fold

2

**Shoe**
Cut 1 black solid

1

**Frame**
Cut 1 blue print

Place line on fold

# Garden Stars

By Judith Sandstrom

*Colorful fabrics combine to create star blocks pretty enough to be flowers in a garden.*

## Project Specifications

**Skill Level:** Beginner
**Project Size:** 62 1/2" x 73"
**Block Size:** 10 1/2" x 10 1/2"
**Number of Blocks:** 30

## Materials

- 1/2 yard each purple, yellow, blue and red tone-on-tone prints
- 1 yard yellow floral print
- 1 yard green tone-on-tone print
- 2 yards cream-on-cream print
- Backing 66" x 77"
- Batting 66" x 77"
- 8 yards self-made or purchased binding
- Neutral color all-purpose thread
- White quilting thread
- Basic sewing supplies and tools

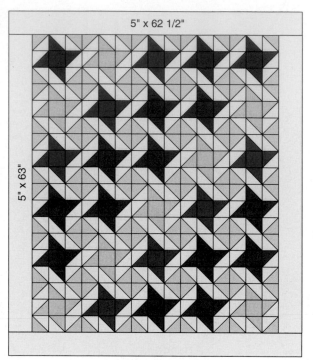

**Garden Stars**
Placement Diagram
62 1/2" x 73"

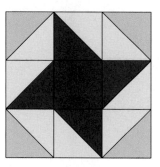

**Garden Stars**
10 1/2" x 10 1/2" Block

## Instructions

**Step 1.** Cut 14 strips cream-on-cream print and seven strips green tone-on-tone print 4 3/8" by fabric width; subcut into 4 3/8" square segments. You will need 120 cream-on-cream print squares and 60 green tone-on-tone print squares. Cut each square in half on one diagonal to make A triangles.

**Step 2.** Cut one strip each purple, yellow, blue and red tone-on-tone prints 4" by fabric width;

subcut into 4" square segments. You will need eight purple and yellow and seven blue and red segments for B.

**Step 3.** Cut two strips each purple, yellow, blue and red tone-on-tone prints 4 3/8" by fabric width; subcut into 4 3/8" square segments. Cut each segment in half on one diagonal to make A triangles. You will need 32 purple and yellow and 28 blue and red triangles for A.

**Step 4.** Sew a cream-on-cream print A triangle to each colored A triangle as shown in Figure 1.

Make 120   Make 28   Make 32   Make 28   Make 32

**Figure 1**
Sew a cream-on-cream print A triangle
to a colored A triangle as shown.

*Garden Stars continued on page 129*

# Table Tulips

By Marian Shenk

*Piecing and appliqué combine to make this table mat using spring colors.*

## Project Specifications

**Skill Level:** Intermediate

**Table Mat Size:** 12" x 22 1/2"

**Block Size:** 12" x 12"

**Number of Blocks:** 1

## Materials

- 1 fat quarter each light peach print and green solid
- 1/4 yard each teal and dark peach prints
- 1/2 yard white-on-white print
- Backing 16" x 26"
- Batting 16" x 26"
- 2 1/2 yards self-made or purchased binding
- All-purpose thread to match fabrics
- Off-white quilting thread
- Basic sewing supplies and tools

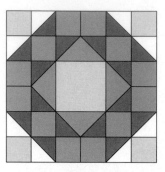

**Broken Dishes Variation**
12" x 12" Block

## Instructions

**Step 1.** Prepare templates for all pieces using pattern pieces given; cut as directed on each piece, adding a seam allowance to all appliqué pieces for hand appliqué.

**Step 2.** To piece the Broken Dishes Variation block, sew a dark peach B to each short side

of C as shown in Figure 1; repeat for four units. Join two teal print A pieces and sew to the B side of the B-C unit; repeat for four units.

**Figure 1**
Sew a dark peach B to
each short side of C.

**Step 3.** Sew a white-on-white print B to a dark peach B along the diagonal; repeat for eight units. Sew a B unit to a light peach A square and a B unit to a teal print A square as shown in Figure 2. Join the two A-B units to make a corner square as shown in Figure 3; repeat for four corner squares.

**Figure 2**
Sew a B unit to a light peach A
square and a B unit to a teal
print A square as shown.

**Figure 3**
Join the A-B units to make a
corner square as shown.

**Step 4.** Arrange pieced units with D in rows as shown in Figure 4; join in rows. Join rows to complete the pieced block; press.

**Step 5.** Arrange appliqué pieces on the scallop piece referring to the Placement Diagram and the scallop piece for positioning. Appliqué in place in numerical order using thread to match fabrics referring to Figure 5. ***Note: Trim center stem as necessary to fit on scallop piece.***

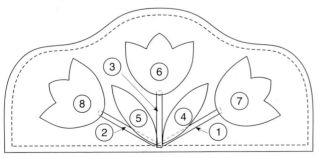

**Figure 5**
Appliqué pieces in place in numerical order as shown.

**Step 6.** Sew a scallop piece to opposite sides of the pieced square.

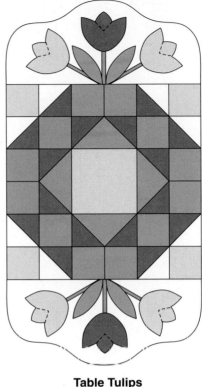

**Table Tulips**
Placement Diagram
12" x 22 1/2"

**Step 7.** Prepare the appliquéd and pieced top for quilting, quilt and bind referring to the General Instructions. ***Note: The table mat shown was hand-quilted in the ditch of seams, around appliqué shapes and using a purchased quilting design in the D square using off-white quilting thread.*** ❧

**Figure 4**
Arrange units in
rows as shown.

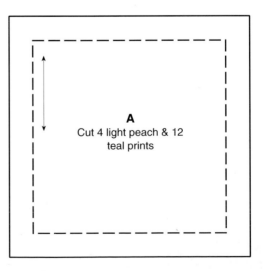

**A**
Cut 4 light peach & 12
teal prints

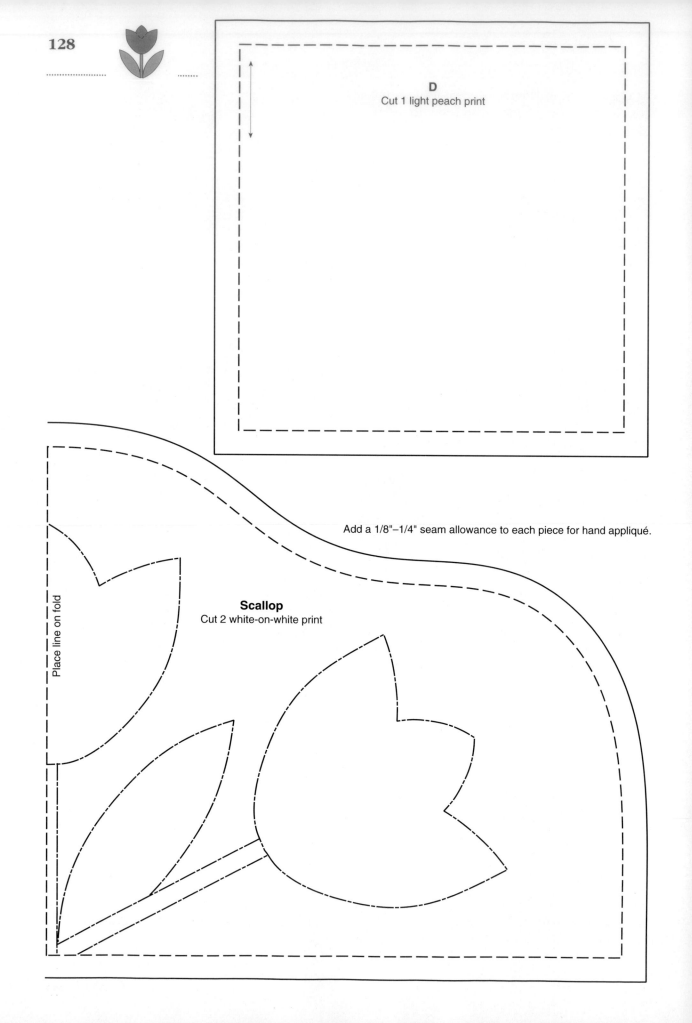

**D**
Cut 1 light peach print

Add a 1/8"–1/4" seam allowance to each piece for hand appliqué.

Place line on fold

**Scallop**
Cut 2 white-on-white print

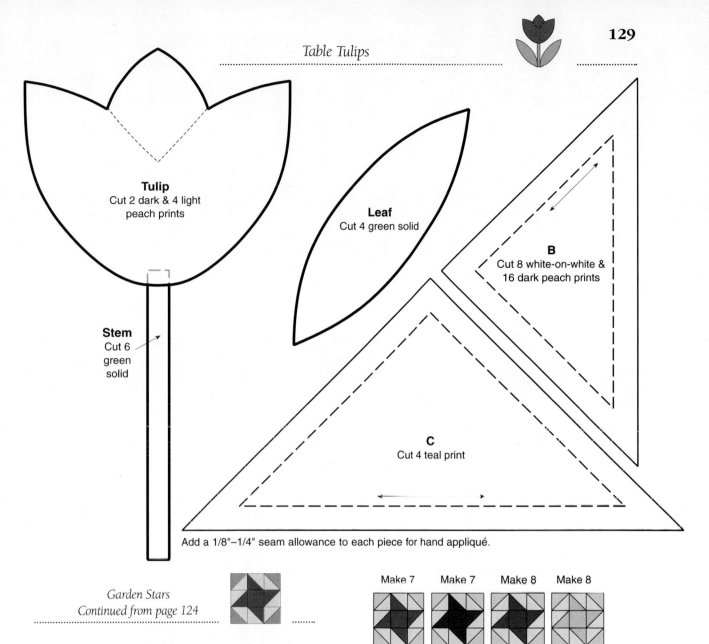

**Tulip**
Cut 2 dark & 4 light
peach prints

**Leaf**
Cut 4 green solid

**B**
Cut 8 white-on-white &
16 dark peach prints

**Stem**
Cut 6
green
solid

**C**
Cut 4 teal print

Add a 1/8"–1/4" seam allowance to each piece for hand appliqué.

---

*Garden Stars
Continued from page 124*

**Step 5.** Join four cream/green A units with a blue tone-on-tone print B and four cream/blue A units to make a block as shown in Figure 2; repeat for seven cream/green/blue blocks.

**Figure 2**
Join 4 cream/green A units with a blue
tone-on-tone print B and 4 cream/blue
A units to make a block as shown.

**Step 6.** Complete seven cream/green/red and eight each cream/green/purple and cream/green/yellow blocks as shown in Figure 3.

Make 7   Make 7   Make 8   Make 8

**Figure 3**
Complete blocks as shown.

**Step 7.** Arrange the blocks in six rows of five blocks each referring to the Placement Diagram for positioning of blocks by color; join blocks in rows. Join rows to complete the pieced center; press seams in one direction.

**Step 8.** Cut and piece two strips each 5 1/2" x 63 1/2" and 5 1/2" x 63" yellow floral print. Sew the longer strips to opposite long sides and shorter strips to the top and bottom; press seams toward strips.

**Step 9.** Prepare for quilting, quilt and bind referring to the General Instructions. ***Note:** The quilt shown was hand-quilted using white quilting thread.* ❧

# Glorious Bed Quilts

Making bed-size quilts in 20 hours or less can be a challenge.

You must have everything ready when you begin. Set aside a whole weekend with nothing else to do but cut and sew.

It helps to cut everything first and stitch all units before assembling any of them, but before you begin, it is always helpful to make a sample block or unit to make sure your sewing is accurate.

Once you have accomplished this, you are ready to begin a weekend of stitching fun. Remember to take breaks to give your body a chance to stretch and relax. You'll come back invigorated and ready to quilt again!

# Campfire Nine-Patch

By Sandra L. Hatch

*Fabric prints inspire designs as much as color and imagination. The fabrics in this quilt include prints with wildlife themes—moose, bears, canoes and more. The bright colors don't reflect a camping look, but would brighten up any camping activity.*

## Project Specifications

**Quilt Size:** 77" x 86"
**Block Size:** 9" x 9"
**Number of Blocks:** 56

## Materials

- 1 strip each red and green prints 2 1/2" by fabric width
- 5/8 yard red print
- 1 yard each green, yellow confetti, yellow-on-yellow and red motif prints
- 1 1/8 yards yellow print
- 1 7/8 yards blue print
- 3 yards large motif print
- Batting 81" x 90"
- Backing 81" x 90"
- 9 1/2 yards self-made or purchased binding
- All-purpose thread to match fabrics
- Basic sewing supplies and tools, rotary cutter, mat and ruler

**Framed Nine-Patch**
9" x 9" Block

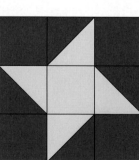

**Spinning Star**
9" x 9" Block

The large motif print used to make this quilt has a definite up-and-down pattern. The side border strips were cut from the length of the fabric. The strips for the top and bottom were cut from the width of the

fabric. When piecing strips for top and bottom borders, the seams can be hidden if the strips are cut from identical motif areas and pieced with the same motifs in the seams. This requires planning when cutting and uses extra fabric.

## Instructions

### Making Framed Nine-Patch Blocks

**Step 1.** Cut eight strips yellow-on-yellow print and 10 strips red motif print 2 5/8" by fabric width.

**Step 2.** Join strips with right sides together along length to make four red/yellow/red and two yellow/red/yellow strip sets; press seams toward darker fabric.

**Step 3.** Subcut each strip set into 2 5/8" segments as shown in Figure 1; you will need 56 red/yellow/red and 28 yellow/red/yellow segments.

**Step 4.** Join two red/yellow/red and one yellow/red/yellow segments as shown in Figure 2 to make a Nine-Patch unit; repeat for 28 Nine-Patch units.

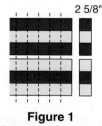

2 5/8"

**Figure 1**
Subcut each strip set into 2 5/8" segments.

**Figure 2**
Join 2 red/yellow/red and 1 yellow/red/yellow segments as shown to make a Nine-Patch unit.

**Step 5.** Cut four strips each yellow confetti and green prints 5 3/8" by fabric width; subcut each strip into 5 3/8" square segments. Cut each square in half to make two triangles; you will need 56 each yellow confetti and green print triangles.

**Step 6.** Sew a yellow confetti print triangle to

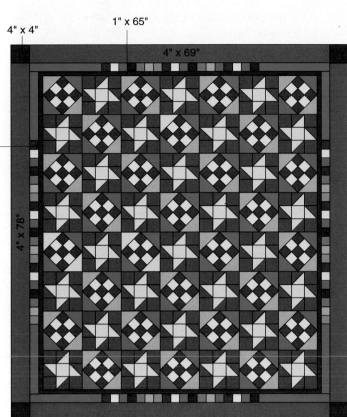

4" x 4"

1" x 65"

4" x 69"

1" x 72"

4" x 78"

**Campfire Nine-Patch**
Placement Diagram
77" x 86"

3 7/8" by fabric width. Subcut each strip into 3 7/8" square segments—you will need 56 squares of each fabric. Cut each square in half on one diagonal to make 112 triangles of each color.

**Step 2.** Sew a blue print triangle to a yellow print triangle along diagonals as shown in Figure 5; repeat for 112 triangle units. Press seams toward blue print triangles; set aside.

**Figure 5**
Sew a blue print triangle
to a yellow print triangle
along diagonals.

**Step 3.** Cut three strips yellow print and 10 strips blue print 3 1/2" by fabric width; subcut each strip into 3 1/2" square segments. You will need 112 blue print and 28 yellow print squares.

**Step 4.** Sew a blue print square to two opposite sides of one blue/yellow triangle/square as shown in Figure 6; repeat for 56 units. Press seams toward blue print squares.

3 1/2" x 3 1/2"

**Figure 6**
Sew a blue print square to 2 opposite
sides of 1 blue/yellow triangle/square.

**Step 5.** Sew a blue/yellow triangle/square to opposite sides of a yellow print square as shown in Figure 7; repeat for 28 units. Press seams toward yellow print square.

**Step 6.** Join the pieced units as shown in Figure 8 to complete one Spinning Star block; repeat for 28 blocks.

opposite sides of one Nine-Patch unit; press seams toward triangles. Sew a green print triangle to the remaining two sides of the Nine-Patch unit to complete one Framed Nine-Patch block as shown in Figure 3; press seams toward green print triangles. Repeat for 28 blocks.

**Step 7.** Trim triangle points off each side of the block as shown in Figure 4; set blocks aside.

**Figure 3**
Sew a green print
triangle to the
remaining 2 sides of
the Nine-Patch unit to
complete 1 Framed
Nine-Patch block.

**Figure 4**
Trim triangle points off each
side of block as shown.

## Making Spinning Star Blocks

**Step 1.** Cut six strips each yellow and blue prints

3 1/2" x 3 1/2"

**Figure 7**
Sew a blue/yellow triangle/square
to opposite sides of a yellow print
square as shown.

**Figure 8**
Join the pieced units as
shown to complete 1
Spinning Star block.

## Constructing Quilt Top

**Step 1.** Join four Spinning Star blocks with three Framed Nine-Patch blocks to make a row, arranging blocks as shown in Figure 9; repeat for four rows. *Note: The placement of the green and yellow confetti print triangles is the same in every row to create a diagonal color arrangement. Press seams in one direction.*

**Figure 9**
Join 4 Spinning Star blocks with 3
Framed Nine-Patch blocks to make a
row, arranging blocks as shown.

**Step 2.** Join four Framed Nine-Patch blocks with three Spinning Star blocks to make a row, arranging blocks as shown in Figure 10; repeat for four rows. Press seams in one direction.

**Figure 10**
Join 4 Framed Nine-Patch blocks with 3
Spinning Star blocks to make a row,
arranging blocks as shown.

**Step 3.** Arrange rows referring to the Placement Diagram for positioning; join rows to complete pieced center. Press seams in one direction.

**Step 4.** Cut and piece two strips each red print 1 1/2" x 65 1/2" and 1 1/2" x 72 1/2"; sew the longer strips to opposite long sides of the pieced center and shorter strips to the top and bottom. Press seams toward strips.

**Step 5.** Cut one strip each red motif, yellow-on-yellow, yellow confetti, green and blue prints 2 1/2" by fabric width.

**Step 6.** Join strips with right sides together along length in any order with the extra 2 1/2" by fabric width strips listed with materials; press seams in one direction.

**Step 7.** Subcut strip set into 2 1/2" segments. Join three segments on short ends to make a 21-segment strip as shown in Figure 11; repeat for four strips.

**Figure 11**
Join 3 segments on short ends
to make a 21-segment strip.

**Step 8.** Cut four strips 2 1/2" x 16 1/2" green print. Sew a strip to opposite short ends of two pieced strips as shown in Figure 12; press. Repeat for second pieced strip.

2 1/2" x 16 1/2"

**Figure 12**
Sew a strip to opposite short ends of 2 pieced strips.

**Step 9.** Sew these pieced strips to opposite long sides of the pieced center; press seams toward red print border strips.

**Step 10.** Remove three segments from each of the remaining 21-segment strips to make 18-segment strips. Cut two strips green print 2 1/2" x 17"; sew a strip to each end of the pieced strips. Sew these strips to the top and bottom of the pieced center; press seams toward red print border strips.

**Step 11.** Cut and piece two strips large motif print 4 1/2" x 69 1/2" from width of fabric and two strips 4 1/2" x 78 1/2" from length of fabric. Cut four squares red print 4 1/2" x 4 1/2". Sew the longer strips to opposite long sides; press seams toward strips. Sew a red print square to each end of the remaining two strips and sew to the top and bottom; press seams toward strips.

**Step 12.** Sandwich batting between the completed top and the prepared backing piece; pin or baste to hold. Quilt as desired. *Note: The sample shown was professionally machine-quilted.*

**Step 13.** Trim backing and batting even with top. Remove pins or basting.

**Step 14.** Bind with self-made or purchased binding to finish. ❧

# Ladybugs in the Nine-Patch

By Vicki Blizzard

*Really large yo-yos create the flowers on this fun ladybug-design quilt.*

## Project Specifications

**Quilt Size:** 61" x 80"
**Block Size:** 15" x 15"
**Number of Blocks:** 12 large

## Materials

- 3/8 yard each gold, purple, peach and blue batiks
- 5/8 yard black batik
- 1 yard each bright yellow and red batiks
- 1 1/4 yards white batik
- 1 1/2 yards lime batik
- Hi-loft batting 65" x 84"
- Backing 65" x 84"
- Neutral and black all-purpose thread
- Neutral and black quilting thread
- Basic sewing supplies and tools, rotary cutter, mat and ruler

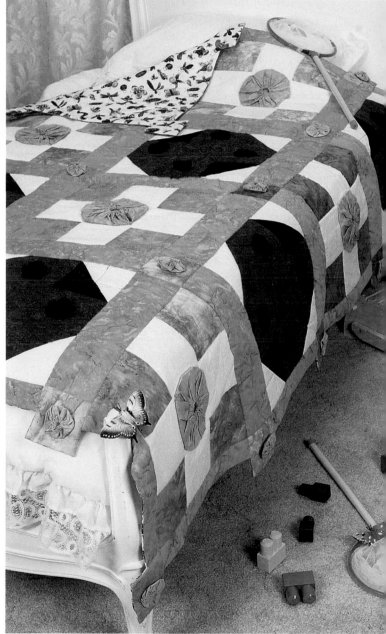

**Nine-Patch**
15" x 15" Block

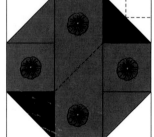

**Ladybug**
15" x 15" Block

## Instructions

### Making Ladybug Blocks

**Step 1.** Cut five strips white batik 5 1/2" by fabric width; subcut two strips into 5 1/2" square segments. You will need 12 white batik squares. Subcut the remaining strips into 15 1/2" segments. You will need 6 white batik rectangles.

**Step 2.** Cut four each gold and purple batiks and eight each blue and peach batiks 5 1/2" x 5 1/2" squares.

**Step 3.** To piece one Nine-Patch block, join two blue batik squares and one white batik square to make a row as shown in Figure 1; repeat for two rows.

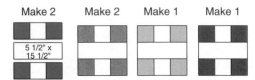

**Figure 1**
To piece 1 Nine-Patch block join 2 blue batik squares and 1 white batik square to make a row.

**Step 4.** Join the rows with a 5 1/2" x 15 1/2" white batik rectangle as shown in Figure 2 to make a blue Nine-Patch block; repeat for two blue, two peach, one gold and one purple Nine-Patch blocks; set aside.

Make 2    Make 2    Make 1    Make 1

5 1/2" x 15 1/2"

**Figure 2**
Join the rows with a 5 1/2" x 15 1/2" rectangle as shown to make a Nine-Patch block.

### Making Ladybug Blocks

**Step 1.** From red batik, cut twelve 5 1/2" x 5 1/2" squares and six 5 1/2" x 15 1/2" rectangles.

**Step 2.** Cut six each black and red batik and twelve white batik squares 5 7/8" x 5 7/8". Cut each square on one diagonal to make triangles. Sew a black triangle to a white triangle as shown in Figure 3; repeat for 12 units. Sew a red triangle to a white triangle; repeat for 12 units.

**Step 3.** Sew a red square between a black/white and a red/white unit to make a row as shown in Figure 4; repeat for two rows.

**Figure 3**
Sew a black triangle to a white triangle.

**Figure 4**
Sew a red square between a black/white and a red/white unit to make a row.

**Step 4.** Join the two rows with a 5 1/2" x 15 1/2" red batik rectangle to complete one block as shown in Figure 5; repeat for six blocks.

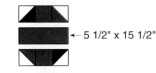
← 5 1/2" x 15 1/2"

**Figure 5**
Join the rows with a 5 1/2" x 15 1/2" rectangle to complete 1 block.

### Completing Quilt Top

**Step 1.** Cut 17 strips lime batik 4 1/2" x 15 1/2" for sashing strips. Cut five each purple, blue, peach

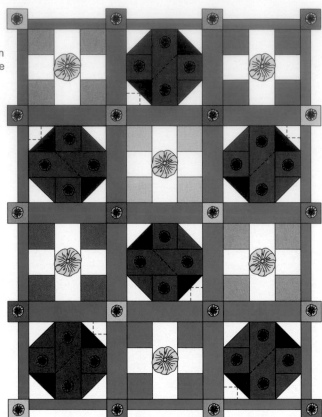

**Ladybugs in the Nine-Patch**
Placement Diagram
61" x 80"

and gold batik 4 1/2" x 4 1/2" sashing squares.

**Step 2.** Cut 14 strips lime batik 2 1/2" x 15 1/2" for border strips.

**Step 3.** Join one of each color sashing square and three 2 1/2" x 15 1/2" border strips to make a row as shown in Figure 6; repeat for two rows, referring to the Placement Diagram for positioning of second row. *Note: The squares are wider than the strips and will extend beyond the strip when stitching.*

4 1/2" x 4 1/2"    2 1/2" x 15 1/2"

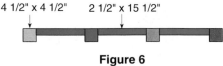

**Figure 6**
Join 4 sashing squares and three 2 1/2" x 15 1/2" border strips to make a row.

**Step 4.** Join three 5 1/2" x 15 1/2" sashing strips with one of each color sashing square, placing squares randomly or referring to the Placement Diagram for color positioning in each row; press seams toward squares; repeat for three sashing rows.

**Step 5.** Join two border strips, two sashing strips, two Nine-Patch blocks and one Ladybug block to make a row as shown in Figure 7; repeat for two rows, placing blocks in a random color placement or referring to the Placement Diagram for positioning of blocks. Press seams toward sashing strips.

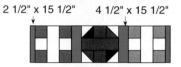

**Figure 7**
Join 2 border strips, 2 sashing strips, 2 Nine-Patch blocks and 1 Ladybug block to make a row.

**Step 6.** Join two border strips, two sashing strips, two Ladybug blocks and one Nine-Patch block to make a row as shown in Figure 8; repeat for two rows, placing blocks in a random color placement or referring to the Placement Diagram for positioning of blocks. Press seams toward sashing strips.

2 1/2" x 15 1/2"    4 1/2" x 15 1/2"

**Figure 8**
Join 2 border strips, 2 sashing strips, 2 Ladybug blocks and 1 Nine-Patch block to make a row.

**Step 7.** Join the block rows and the sashing rows, matching seams of sashing squares and strips and referring to the Placement Diagram for positioning of rows. *Note: The edge squares on each sashing strip will extend beyond border strips.*

**Step 8.** Pin batting to the wrong side of the pieced top. Place layered top right sides together with prepared backing piece; pin or baste layers flat. Trim batting and backing even with quilt top edges.

**Step 9.** Stitch all around edges using a 1/4" seam allowance, leaving a 10" opening between edge squares on one side. Clip corners; turn right side out. Iron edges flat; slipstitch opening closed.

**Step 10.** Prepare template for yo-yo; cut as

directed on the piece. Cut six 13"-diameter circles bright yellow batik.

**Step 11.** Knot the ends of a double strand of matching all-purpose thread, hand-stitch around edge of each circle 1/4" from edge as shown in Figure 9.

**Step 12.** Pull to gather as shown in Figure 10.

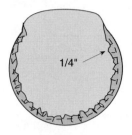

**Figure 9**
Knot the ends of a double strand of matching all-purpose thread; hand-stitch around edge of each circle 1/4" from edge as shown.

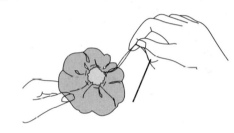

**Figure 10**
Pull to gather as shown.

*Ladybugs in the Nine-Patch continued on page 153*

**Yo-Yo**
Cut 20 bright yellow & 24 black batiks

# Garden Pathways

By Judith Sandstrom

*Looks can be deceiving. This quilt is not made in blocks but rather in sections.*
*Although simple in construction, constructing the top is like putting puzzle pieces together.*

## Project Specifications

**Quilt Size:** 82 3/4" x 102 1/4"

## Materials

- 1/2 yard each purple and lavender prints
- 1 1/8 yards dark green print
- 1 1/4 yards light green print
- 1 1/4 yards green-and-purple print
- 4 1/2 yards cream-on-cream print
- Batting 85" x 106"
- Backing 85" x 106"
- 10 3/4 yards self-made or purchased binding
- All-purpose thread to match fabrics
- Cream quilting thread
- Basic sewing supplies and tools, rotary cutter, mat and ruler

## Instructions

**Step 1.** Cut 33 strips cream-on-cream print 3 3/4" by fabric width; set aside 13 strips. Subcut eight strips into 3 3/4" square segments for A; you will need 84 A squares. Subcut 12 strips into 10 1/4" segments for B; you will need 45 B pieces.

**Step 2.** Cut eight strips each light green and cream-on-cream prints 4 1/8" by fabric width; subcut each strip into 4 1/8" square segments. You will need 80 squares of each fabric. Cut each square in half on one diagonal to make C triangles; you will need 160 C triangles of each fabric.

**Step 3.** Sew a cream-on-cream print C to a light green print C as shown in Figure 1; repeat for all C triangles to make 160 C units. Set aside.

**Figure 1**
Sew a cream-on-cream print
C to a light green print C.

**Step 4.** Join two C units with an A square to make an X unit as shown in Figure 2; repeat for 80 X units.

**Figure 2**
Join 2 C units with an A
square to make an X unit.

**Step 5.** Join B with two X units as shown in Figure 3 to make one Y unit; repeat for 31 Y units.

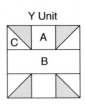

**Figure 3**
Join B with 2 X units
to make a Y unit.

**Step 6.** Cut four strips each purple and lavender prints and nine strips dark green print 3 3/4" by fabric width.

**Step 7.** Join strips with cream-on-cream print strips set aside in Step 1 with right sides together along length in the following color combinations to make strip sets: purple/cream/purple—make 2; lavender/cream/lavender—make 2; dark green/cream/dark green—make 3; and cream/dark green/cream—make 3. Press seams toward darker fabric.

**Step 8.** Subcut each strip set into 3 3/4" segments as shown in Figure 4.

**Step 9.** Join segments to make Nine-Patch units as shown in Figure 5.

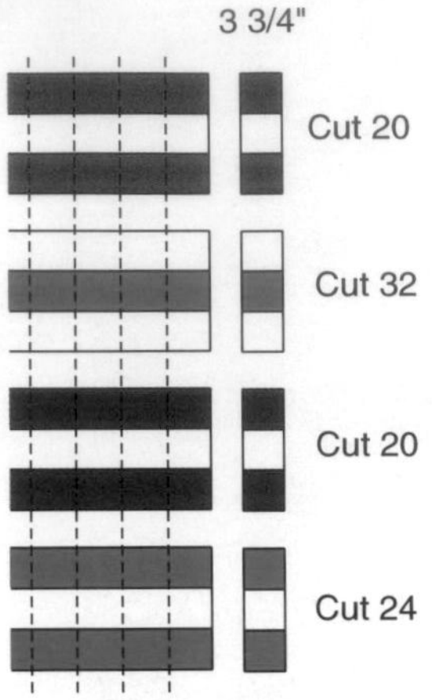

*Garden Pathways*

3 3/4"

Cut 20

Cut 32

Cut 20

Cut 24

**Figure 4**
Subcut each strip set
into 3 3/4" segments.

Make 10     Make 10     Make 12

**Figure 5**
Join segments to make
Nine-Patch units as shown.

4" x 4"

4" x 74 3/4"

4" x 94 1/4"

**Garden Pathways**
Placement Diagram
82 3/4" x 102 1/4"

**Step 10.** Referring to Figure 6, arrange and join pieces and units in horizontal rows; press seams open.

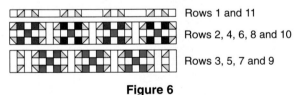

Rows 1 and 11

Rows 2, 4, 6, 8 and 10

Rows 3, 5, 7 and 9

**Figure 6**
Arrange and join pieces and units in horizontal rows.

**Step 11.** Arrange the pieced rows in numerical order referring to the Placement Diagram for positioning of rows; join rows to complete the pieced center. Press seams open.

**Step 12.** Cut and piece two strips each green-and-purple print 4 1/2" x 75 1/4" and 4 1/2" x 94

3/4" and four squares dark green print 4 1/2" x 4 1/2". Sew the longer strips to opposite long sides of the pieced center; press seams toward strips. Sew a square to each end of the remaining two strips; sew to the top and bottom of the pieced center. Press seams toward strips.

**Step 13.** Sandwich batting between the completed top and the prepared backing piece; pin or baste to hold. Quilt as desired. *Note: The sample shown was hand-quilted using cream quilting thread.*

**Step 14.** Trim backing and batting even with top. Remove pins or basting.

**Step 15.** Bind with self-made or purchased binding to finish. ❧

# Rose Garden
By Sue Harvey

*Traditional Rolling Nine-Patch blocks take on the look of roses in this twin-size bed quilt. Careful placement of the light and dark values of pink and purple gives the effect of flower centers and outer petals.*

## Project Specifications

**Quilt Size:** 70" x 84 3/8"
**Block Size:** 11 7/8" x 11 7/8"
**Number of Blocks:** 20

## Materials

- 1/2 yard pink print
- 1/2 yard lavender print
- 1 yard purple print
- 1 yard burgundy print
- 2 yards pastel mottled
- 2 1/8 yards navy print
- 2 1/4 yards roses print
- Backing 74" x 89"
- Batting 74" x 89"
- All-purpose thread to match fabrics
- Basic sewing tools and supplies, rotary cutter, mat and ruler

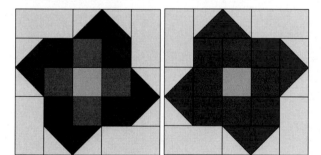

**Rolling Nine-Patch**
11 7/8" x 11 7/8" Block

**Reversed Rolling Nine-Patch**
11 7/8" x 11 7/8" Block

## Instructions

**Step 1.** Cut four strips each 2 7/8" by fabric width pink, lavender, purple and burgundy prints. Cut two strips 2 7/8" by fabric width roses print.

**Step 2.** To make Nine-Patch centers, sew a pink print strip between two burgundy print strips to make an A strip set; repeat for two A strip sets. Sew a roses print strip between two pink print

strips to make a B strip set. Cut strip sets into 2 7/8" segments as shown in Figure 1. You will need 20 A segments and 10 B segments.

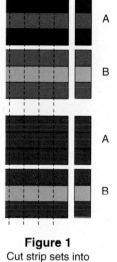

**Figure 1**
Cut strip sets into
2 7/8" segments.

**Step 3.** Sew a B segment between two A segments to complete one Nine-Patch center as shown in Figure 2. Repeat to make 10 burgundy Nine-Patch centers.

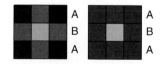

**Figure 2**
Sew a B segment between
2 A segments to complete 1
Nine-Patch center.

**Step 4.** Repeat Steps 2 and 3 to make 10 purple Nine-Patch centers using lavender, purple and roses print strips.

**Step 5.** Cut three strips each 5 1/4" by fabric width purple and burgundy prints; subcut each strip into 2 7/8" segments for C. You will need 40 C segments of each color.

**Step 6.** Cut 12 strips 2 7/8" by fabric width

5" x 70"

2 1/2" x 60"

5" x 74 3/8"

2 1/2" x 69 3/8"

**Rose Garden**
Placement Diagram
70" x 84 3/8"

pastel mottled; subcut each strip into 2 7/8" square segments for D. You will need 160 D squares. Draw a diagonal line on the wrong side of each D square.

**Step 7.** To make Flying Geese units, place a D square right sides together on one end of a burgundy print C segment as shown in Figure 3. Stitch on the diagonal line, trim to a 1/4" seam allowance and press D open as shown in Figure 4. Repeat on the opposite end of C as shown in Figure 5 to complete one Flying Geese unit. Repeat with all C segments to make 40 each burgundy and purple Flying Geese units.

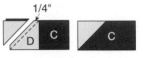

**Figure 3**
Place a D square on 1
end of a C segment.

**Figure 4**
Stitch on the diagonal;
trim seam allowance
and press D open.

**Figure 5**
Repeat on the
opposite end of C.

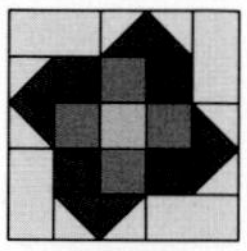

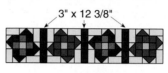

**Step 8.** Cut six strips 5 1/4" by fabric width pastel mottled; subcut each strip into 2 7/8" segments for E. You will need 80 E segments.

**Step 9.** To piece one burgundy Rolling Nine-Patch block, sew an E segment to one end of a burgundy Flying Geese unit to make a block unit as shown in Figure 6; repeat for four block units.

**Figure 6**
Sew E to 1 end of a
burgundy Flying Geese unit.

**Step 10.** Place a block unit right sides together with a burgundy Nine-Patch center as shown in Figure 7. Stitch a partial seam, stopping 1/2" from end of Nine-Patch center as shown in Figure 8.

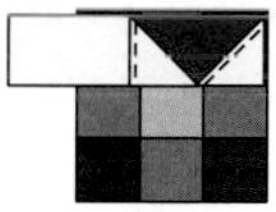

**Figure 7**
Place a block unit right sides
together with a burgundy
Nine-Patch center.

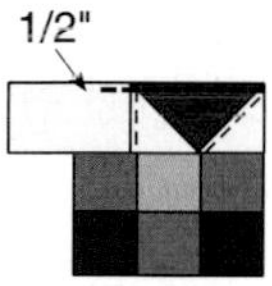

**Figure 8**
Stitch stopping 1/2" from
end of Nine-Patch center.

**Step 11.** Place a second block unit on the adjacent side of the Nine-Patch center; stitch. Continue adding block units to the Nine-Patch center, completing the partial seam when all block units have been added as shown in Figure 9.

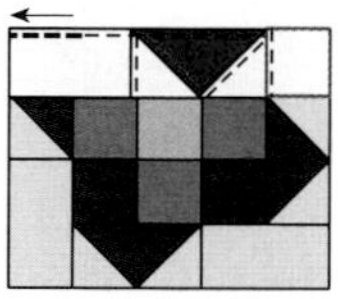

**Figure 9**
Complete beginning partial
seam as shown.

**Step 12.** Repeat Steps 9–11 to complete 10 each burgundy and purple Rolling Nine-Patch blocks referring to the block drawing for placement of pieces in the purple blocks.

**Step 13.** Cut two strips each navy print 3" x 60 1/2" and 3" x 69 7/8" from length of fabric; set aside for borders. Cut 31 strips 3" x 12 3/8"

for sashing strips from remaining fabric width.

**Step 14.** Cut two strips each roses print 5 1/2" x 70 1/2" and 5 1/2" x 74 7/8" from length of fabric; set aside for borders. Cut 12 squares 3" x 3" for sashing squares.

**Step 15.** Join two each burgundy and purple blocks with three sashing strips as shown in Figure 10; repeat for five block rows.

3" x 12 3/8"

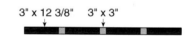

**Figure 10**
Join 2 each burgundy and purple blocks
with sashing strips to make a block row.

**Step 16.** Join four sashing strips with three sashing squares to make a sashing row as shown in Figure 11; repeat for four sashing rows.

3" x 12 3/8"    3" x 3"

**Figure 11**
Join 4 sashing strips with 3 sashing
squares to make a sashing row.

**Step 17.** Arrange block rows with sashing rows referring to the Placement Diagram for positioning of rows. Join rows to complete the pieced center.

**Step 18.** Sew the longer navy print border strips to opposite sides of the pieced center; press seams toward strips. Sew the shorter strips to the top and bottom; press seams toward strips.

**Step 19.** Repeat Step 18 with the roses print strips to complete the pieced top.

**Step 20.** Sandwich the pieced top with the prepared backing and batting pieces; pin or baste to hold. Quilt as desired.

**Step 21.** Cut 12 strips 2 1/4" by remaining fabric width navy print. Join on short ends to make one long strip. Fold in half with wrong sides together; press. Bind quilt. *Note: You will need approximately 8 3/4 yards of binding.* ➤

# Sunflower Patch

By Judith Sandstrom

*Sunflower prints have been popular for many years. This quilt takes advantage of pretty fall colors and a simple pieced block to make a cheerful bed cover.*

## Project Specifications

**Quilt Size:** 75" x 90"

**Block Size:** 12" x 12"

**Number of Blocks:** 20

## Materials

- 1 yard each brown, yellow and gold prints
- 1 1/2 yards sunflower print
- 2 5/8 yards green print
- Batting 79" x 94"
- Backing 79" x 94"
- 9 1/2 yards self-made or purchased binding
- All-purpose thread to match fabrics
- Cream quilting thread
- Basic sewing supplies and tools, rotary cutter, mat and ruler

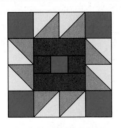

**Sunflower Patch**
12" x 12" Block

## Instructions

**Step 1.** Cut 24 strips green print 3 1/2" by fabric width. Leave 14 strips whole except cut 12 1/2" off one strip; cut five strips into fifteen 12 1/2" sashing strips; and cut five strips into eighty 2 1/2" square segments for A.

**Step 2.** Cut eight strips each yellow and gold prints 3 7/8" by fabric width. Subcut each strip into 3 7/8" square segments; cut each square on one diagonal to make B triangles. You will need 160 B triangles of each color.

**Step 3.** Sew a gold print B to a yellow print B as shown in Figure 1; repeat for all B triangles. Set aside.

**Figure 1**
Sew a gold print B
to a yellow print B.

**Step 4.** Cut 11 strips brown print 2 1/2" by fabric width; cut seven of the strips into forty 6 1/2" C strips. Set aside the remaining four strips.

**Step 5.** Cut two strips green print 2 1/2" by fabric width. Sew a green print strip between two brown print strips with right sides together along length; repeat for two strip sets. Press seams toward brown print strips.

**Step 6.** Subcut strips into 2 1/2" segments as shown in Figure 2. Sew a C strip to opposite long sides of a pieced segment as shown in Figure 3; repeat for 20 pieced C units.

**Figure 2**
Subcut strip sets into
2 1/2" segments.

**Figure 3**
Sew a C strip to opposite
long sides of a pieced
segment as shown.

**Step 7.** Join two B units as shown in Figure 4; repeat for 80 B units.

**Figure 4**
Join 2 B units as shown.

**Step 8.** Sew a B unit to opposite sides of a C unit as shown in Figure 5; repeat for 20 units.

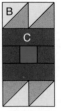

**Figure 5**
Sew a B unit to opposite
sides of a C unit.

**Step 9.** Sew an A square to each end of the remaining B units as shown in Figure 6. Sew two

A-B units to a pieced B-C unit to complete one block as shown in Figure 7; repeat for 20 blocks.

**Figure 6**
Sew an A square to each end of the remaining B units.

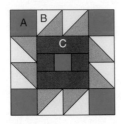

**Figure 7**
Sew 2 A-B units to a pieced B-C unit to complete 1 block.

**Step 10.** Join five blocks with four green print sashing strips to make a block row as shown in Figure 8; repeat for four block rows. Press seams toward strips.

**Step 11.** Cut and piece two strips green print
3 1/2" x 63 1/2" and five strips 3 1/2" x 72 1/2" from strips cut in Step 1. Join the block rows with the longer strips, beginning and ending with a strip; press seams toward strips. Sew the shorter strips to the top and bottom.

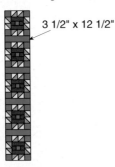

3 1/2" x 12 1/2"

**Figure 8**
Join 5 blocks with 4 green print sashing strips to make a block row.

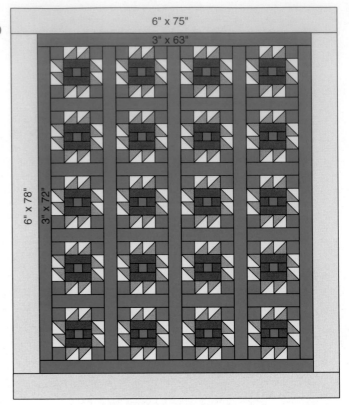

6" x 75"

3" x 63"

6" x 78"

3" x 72"

**Sunflower Patch**
Placement Diagram
75" x 90"

**Step 12.** Cut and piece two strips each sunflower print 6 1/2" x 75 1/2" and 6 1/2" x 78 1/2". Sew the longer strips to opposite long sides and shorter strips to the top and bottom of the pieced center; press seams toward strips.

**Step 13.** Sandwich batting between the completed top and the prepared backing piece; pin or baste to hold. Quilt as desired. *Note: The sample shown was hand-quilted using cream quilting thread.*

**Step 14.** Trim backing and batting even with top. Remove pins or basting.

**Step 15.** Bind with self-made or purchased binding to finish. ❧

# Wisteria Stars

By Sue Harvey

*This king-size bed quilt goes together in a hurry with strip piecing in big 30" blocks. The unpieced center squares provide a perfect showcase for a large floral motif, adding sophistication to the geometric design.*

## Project Specifications

**Quilt Size:** 105" x 105"

**Block Size:** 30" x 30"

**Number of Blocks:** 9

## Materials

- 1 yard large floral print
- 1 yard cream floral print
- 1 yard green mottled
- 3 yards purple print
- 2 3/8 yards gold print
- 3 yards cream mottled
- 4 yards green floral print
- Batting 109" x 109"
- Backing 109" x 109"
- 12 1/4 yards self-made or purchased binding
- All-purpose thread to match fabrics
- Basic sewing supplies and tools, rotary cutter, mat and ruler

**Wisteria Stars**
Placement Diagram
105" x 105"

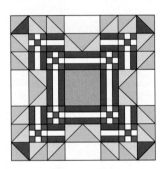

**Cubes and Bars**
30" x 30" Block

## Instructions

**Step 1.** Cut four strips 4 1/4" x 83" from length of green floral print; set aside for borders.

**Step 2.** Cut 17 strips 4 5/8" x 25" from remaining width and two strips 4 5/8" by full fabric width green floral print; subcut each strip into 4 5/8" square segments for A. You will need 96 green A squares.

**Step 3.** Cut five strips 8" by full fabric width green floral print; subcut into 4 1/4" segments for B. You will need 44 B rectangles.

**Step 4.** Cut four squares 4 1/4" x 4 1/4" green floral print for F; set aside for use in borders.

**Step 5.** Cut three strips 4 5/8" by fabric width purple print; subcut each strip into 4 5/8"

square segments for A. You will need 24 purple A squares.

**Step 6.** Cut eight strips 4 5/8" by fabric width gold print; subcut each strip into 4 5/8" square segments for A. You will need 72 gold A squares.

**Step 7.** Draw a line on the diagonal on the wrong side of each purple and gold A square as shown in Figure 1.

**Figure 1**
Draw a line on the diagonal on
the wrong side of each purple
and gold A square.

**Step 8.** Place a purple A square right sides together with a green A square. Sew 1/4" away from each side of the drawn line as shown in Figure 2; cut apart on the drawn line and press open to make 2 purple/green A units as shown in Figure 3. Repeat for 48 purple/green A units and 144 gold/green A units.

1/4"

**Figure 2**
Sew 1/4" away from each
side of the drawn line.

**Figure 3**
Cut apart and press open.

**Step 9.** Cut 10 strips 4 1/4" by fabric width gold print; subcut each strip into 4 1/4" square segments for C. You will need 96 C squares.

**Step 10.** Draw a diagonal line on the wrong side of each C square. Place a C square right sides together on one corner of a B rectangle as shown in Figure 4. Sew on the drawn line; trim seam allowance to 1/4" and press C open as shown in Figure 5. Repeat on the opposite end of B to complete one B-C unit as shown in Figure 6; repeat to make 44 B-C units. Set aside remaining C squares for use in borders.

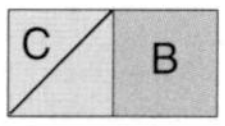

**Figure 4**
Place a C square right sides together
on 1 corner of B as shown.

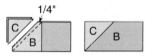

**Figure 5**
Trim seam allowance to 1/4"; press C open.

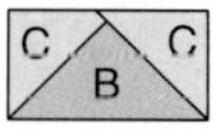

**Figure 6**
Complete 1 B-C
unit as shown.

**Step 11.** Cut eight strips 1 3/4" x 83" from length of purple print; set aside for borders.

**Step 12.** Cut four strips 1 3/4" x 83" from length of cream mottled; set aside for borders.

**Step 13.** Cut 48 strips 1 3/4" x 28" from remaining purple print. Cut 24 strips 1 3/4" x 28" from remaining width cream mottled.

**Step 14.** Sew a cream mottled strip between two purple print strips to make a strip set; repeat with all strips to make 24 strip sets. Press seams toward purple print strips. Cut 12 strip sets into 8" segments and 12 strip sets into 4 1/4" segments as shown in Figure 7. You

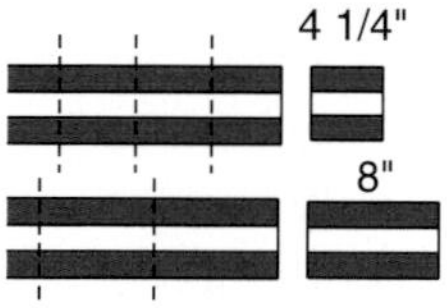

**Figure 7**
Cut strip sets into 8"
and 4 1/4" segments.

will need thirty-six 8" segments and seventy-two 4 1/4" segments.

**Step 15.** Cut 12 strips 1 3/4" by full fabric width cream mottled and 15 strips 1 3/4" by fabric width green mottled.

**Step 16.** Sew a cream mottled strip between two green mottled strips to make a strip set; repeat for six strip sets. Press seams toward

green mottled strips. Cut each set into 1 3/4" segments as shown in Figure 8. You will need 144 green/cream/green segments.

**Step 17.** Sew a green mottled strip between two cream mottled strips to make a strip set; repeat for three strip sets. Press seams toward green mottled strip. Cut each set into 1 3/4" segments again referring to Figure 8. You will need 72 cream/green/cream segments.

**Step 18.** Sew a cream/green/cream segment between two green/cream/green segments to make a Nine-Patch unit as shown in Figure 9; press seams toward center segment. Repeat for 72 Nine-Patch units.

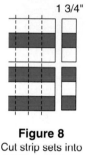

**Figure 8**
Cut strip sets into
1 3/4" segments.

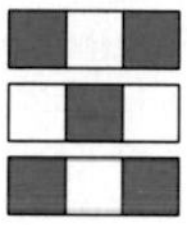

**Figure 9**
Join segments to make
a Nine-Patch unit.

**Step 19.** Cut four strips 8" by fabric width cream floral print; subcut each strip into 4 1/4" segments for D. You will need 36 D rectangles.

**Step 20.** Cut nine squares 8" x 8" large floral print for E, centering a floral motif in each square if desired.

**Step 21.** To piece one Cubes and Bars block, sew D to the B side and an 8" stripe segment to the C side of a B-C unit as shown in Figure 10; repeat for four B-C-D units.

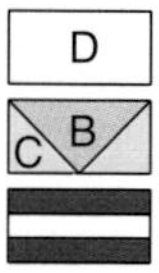

**Figure 10**
Sew D to B-C; add an 8"
stripe segment to
complete 1 B-C-D unit.

**Step 22.** Sew a Nine-Patch unit to a 4 1/4" stripe segment; repeat. Join the two Nine-Patch/stripe units as shown in Figure 11. Repeat for four Nine-Patch/stripe units.

**Figure 11**
Join 2 Nine-Patch/stripe
units as shown.

**Step 23.** Join two gold/green A units as shown in Figure 12; repeat for four A strips and four reversed A strips. Sew an A strip to one side of each Nine-Patch/stripe unit as shown in Figure 13.

Make 4

Make 4

**Figure 12**
Join 2 gold/green
A units as shown.

**Figure 13**
Sew an A strip to 1 side of
a Nine-Patch/stripe unit.

**Step 24.** Sew a purple/green A unit to one end of each reversed A strip as shown in Figure 14. Sew a resulting strip to the adjacent side of each Nine-Patch/stripe unit as shown in Figure 15.

**Figure 14**
Sew a purple/green
A unit to 1 end of a
reversed A strip.

**Figure 15**
Sew a reversed A strip to
the adjacent side of the
Nine-Patch/stripe unit.

**Step 25.** Join two Nine-Patch/stripe units with a B-C-D unit to make a row as shown in Figure 16; repeat. Join two B-C-D units with an E square to make a row, again referring to Figure 16. Join the rows to complete one block, referring to the block drawing for positioning of rows. Repeat Steps 21–25 to make nine blocks.

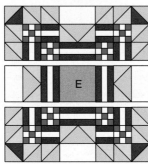

**Figure 16**
Join units with an E square to
make block rows as shown.

**Step 26.** Join three blocks to make a row referring to the Placement Diagram for positioning; repeat for three rows. Join the rows to complete the pieced center.

**Step 27.** Sew a cream mottled border strip between two purple print border strips; press seams toward purple print strips. Repeat for four striped borders.

**Step 28.** Place a C square right sides together on one end of a striped border as shown in Figure 17; sew on the drawn line. Trim seam allowance to 1/4" and press C open as shown

in Figure 18. Repeat on opposite end as shown in Figure 19. Repeat on all striped borders.

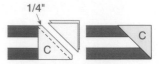

**Figure 17**
Place a C square right
sides together on 1 end
of a striped border.

**Figure 18**
Trim seam allowance
to 1/4"; press C open.

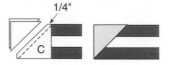

**Figure 19**
Sew C to opposite end of
striped border as shown.

**Step 29.** Sew a purple/green A unit to each end of each striped border as shown in Figure 20. Sew a striped border to opposite sides of the pieced center; press seams toward striped borders.

**Step 30.** Sew a purple/green A unit to each end of each remaining striped border as shown in Figure 21. Sew a striped border to remaining sides of the pieced center, referring to the Placement Diagram for positioning of striped borders.

**Figure 20**
Sew a purple/green A unit to
each end of a striped border.

**Figure 21**
Sew a purple/green
A unit to each end of
the remaining
striped borders.

**Step 31.** Sew a B-C unit to each end of each green floral print strip cut in Step 1 referring to the Placement Diagram for positioning of the B-C units. Sew a strip to opposite sides of the pieced-and-bordered center.

**Step 32.** Sew an F square to each end of the remaining strips; sew a strip to remaining sides of the center to complete the pieced top.

**Step 33.** Sandwich batting between the completed top and the prepared backing piece; pin or baste to hold. Quilt as desired. *Note: The sample shown was professionally machine-quilted.*

**Step 34.** Trim backing and batting even with top. Remove pins or basting.

**Step 35.** Bind with self-made or purchased binding to finish. ❧

# Purple Fancy

By Sandra L. Hatch

*One simple block can be changed or moved around to create so many different designs. This easy block creates several different designs when stitched together.*

## Project Specifications

**Quilt Size:** 68" x 76"

**Block Size:** 8" x 8"

**Number of Blocks:** 56

## Materials

- 3/4 yard each cream, cream-with-purple and purple-with-cream prints
- 3 yards purple print
- 3 5/8 yards brown print
- Batting 72" x 80"
- Backing 72" x 80"
- 8 1/2 yards self-made or purchased binding
- All-purpose thread to match fabrics
- Purple variegated machine-quilting thread
- Basic sewing supplies and tools, rotary cutter, mat and ruler

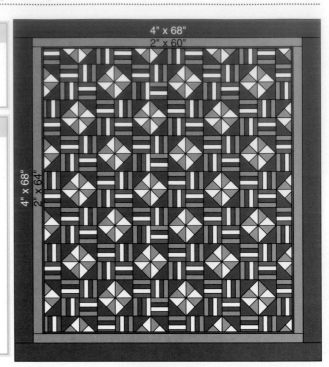

**Purple Fancy**
Placement Diagram
68" x 76"

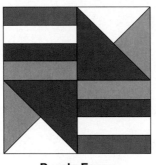

**Purple Fancy**
8" x 8" Block

## Instructions

**Step 1.** Cut 13 strips each 1 1/2" by fabric width purple-with-cream, cream-with-purple, brown and purple prints.

**Step 2.** Join one of each color strip in the color order given with right sides together along length to make a strip set; press seams in one direction. Repeat for 13 strip sets.

**Step 3.** Subcut each strip set into 4 1/2" segments for Unit 1 as shown in Figure 1; you will need 112 Unit 1 segments. Set aside units.

Unit 1
4 1/2"

**Figure 1**
Subcut each strip set into 4 1/2"
segments for Unit 1.

**Step 4.** Cut four strips each cream and purple prints 5 1/4" by fabric width; subcut each strip into 5 1/4" square segments. You will need 28 squares. Cut each square in half on both diagonals to make A triangles; you will need 112 A triangles of each color.

**Step 5.** Sew a cream print A triangle to a purple print A triangle as shown in Figure 2; repeat for all cream and purple print A triangles.

**Step 6.** Cut seven strips brown print 4 7/8" by fabric width; subcut strips into 4 7/8" square segments. You will need 56 squares. Cut each square in half on one diagonal to make B triangles; you will need 112 B triangles.

**Step 7.** Sew an A unit to B to complete Unit 2 as shown in Figure 3; repeat for 112 units.

Unit 2

**Figure 2**
Sew a cream print A
triangle to a purple print
A triangle as shown.

**Figure 3**
Sew an A unit to B to
complete Unit 2 as shown.

**Step 8.** Sew Unit 1 to Unit 2 as shown in Figure 4; repeat for 112 units. Join two units to complete one block as shown in Figure 5; repeat for 56 blocks.

Unit 1  Unit 2

**Figure 4**
Sew Unit 1 to
Unit 2 as shown.

**Figure 5**
Join 2 units to
complete 1 block.

**Step 9.** Join seven blocks for Row 1 as shown in Figure 6; repeat for four rows.

**Figure 6**
Join 7 blocks for Row 1.

**Step 10.** Join seven blocks for Row 2 as shown in Figure 7; repeat for four rows.

**Figure 7**
Join 7 blocks for Row 2.

**Step 11.** Join Rows 1 and 2 as shown in Figure 8; repeat for four row units. Join the row units to complete the pieced top; press seams in one direction.

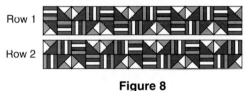

Row 1

Row 2

**Figure 8**
Join Rows 1 and 2 as shown.

**Step 12.** Cut two strips each 1 1/2" x 56 1/2" and 1 1/2" x 64 1/2" brown print. Fold each strip with wrong sides together along length; press.

**Step 13.** Place the shorter strips with right sides together along top and bottom of pieced top; stitch in place. Repeat with longer strips on opposite long sides. *Note: This strip does not add any size to the quilt top. It is an uncorded piping added for a color break.*

**Step 14.** Cut two strips each purple print 2 1/2" x 60 1/2" and 2 1/2" x 64 1/2". Sew the longer strips to opposite long sides and shorter strips to the top and bottom; press seams toward strips.

**Step 15.** Cut four strips brown print 4 1/2" x 68 1/2". Sew a strip to opposite long sides and remaining strips to the top and bottom of the pieced center; press seams toward strips.

**Step 16.** Sandwich batting between the completed top and the prepared backing piece; pin or baste to hold. Quilt as desired. *Note: The sample shown was professionally machine-quilted using purple variegated machine-quilting thread.*

**Step 17.** Trim backing and batting even with top. Remove pins or basting.

**Step 18.** Bind with self-made or purchased binding to finish. ❧

*Ladybugs in the Nine-Patch*
*Continued from page 137*

**Step 13.** Pull the knotted end and the needle end of the thread out about 3" each as shown in Figure 11; cut off needle end.

**Step 14.** Tie a square knot as shown in Figure 12 and then knot once again to secure yo-yo. Cut off both ends of thread, leaving a small tail.

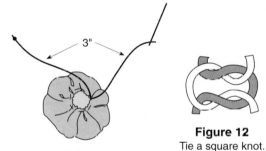

3"

**Figure 12**
Tie a square knot.

**Figure 11**
Pull the knotted end and the needle
end of the thread out about 3" each.

**Step 15.** Stitch four black yo-yos to each Ladybug block referring to Figure 13. Stitch a small bright yellow yo-yo in each sashing square. Stitch a large bright yellow yo-yo to the center of each Nine-Patch block.

**Step 16.** Machine-quilt in the ditch of block and sashing seams using thread to match fabrics. Stitch antennae lines on each Ladybug block using black all-purpose thread and referring to Figure 14 for positioning. ❧

**Figure 13**
Stitch 4 black yo-yos to
each Ladybug block.

**Figure 14**
Stitch antennae lines on
each Ladybug block.

# Prairie Pansies

By Sue Harvey

*This floral-theme quilt uses a traditional block called Prairie Flower.*
*Simply adding block units to the sashing creates an allover flower pattern.*

## Project Specifications

**Quilt Size:** 56" x 88"

**Block Size:** 12" x 12"

**Number of Blocks:** 15

## Materials

- 3/8 yard each pink and purple prints
- 1/2 yard small pansy print
- 1 yard green mottled
- 2 yards stripe
- 3 1/4 yards large pansy print
- Batting 60" x 92"
- Backing 60" x 92"
- 8 1/2 yards self-made or purchased binding
- All-purpose thread to match fabrics
- Basic sewing tools and supplies, rotary cutter, mat and ruler

**Prairie Flower**
12" x 12" Block

## Instructions

**Step 1.** Cut two strips each pink and purple prints 4 1/2" by fabric width; subcut each strip into 4 1/2" square segments. You will need 16 squares each color for A.

**Step 2.** Cut seven strips green mottled 4 1/2" by fabric width; subcut each strip into 4 1/2" square segments. You will need 60 squares for B.

**Step 3.** Cut 14 strips stripe 4 1/2" by fabric width; subcut each strip into 4 1/2" square segments. You will need 124 squares for C.

**Step 4.** Cut three strips small pansy print 4 1/2" by fabric width; subcut each strip into 4 1/2" square segments. You will need 27 squares for D.

**Step 5.** Cut two strips each 2 1/2" x 48 1/2" and 2 1/2" x 76 1/2" large pansy print along length of fabric; set aside for borders.

**Step 6.** Cut 30 strips large pansy print 2 1/2" by

**Prairie Pansies**
Placement Diagram
56" x 88"

remaining fabric width and five strips 2 1/2" by full fabric width; subcut each strip into 2 1/2" square segments. You will need 432 squares for E.

**Step 7.** Cut five strips large pansy print 4 1/2" by fabric width; subcut into 10 sashing squares 4 1/2" x 4 1/2" and 12 sashing segments 4 1/2" x 8 1/2".

**Step 8.** Draw a diagonal line on the wrong side of each E square.

**Step 9.** Place E on one corner of A as shown in Figure 1. Stitch on the diagonal line, trim to a 1/4" seam allowance and press E open as shown in Figure 2. Repeat on an adjacent corner of A as shown in Figure 3. Repeat with all A and C squares.

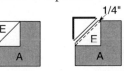

**Figure 1**
Place E on 1 corner of A.

**Figure 2**
Stitch on the diagonal line; trim seam allowance and press E open.

**Figure 3**
Repeat on adjacent corner of A.

**Step 10.** Repeat Step 9 on two opposite corners of each B square as shown in Figure 4.

**Step 11.** To piece one Prairie Flower block, sew a C-E unit between two B-E units as shown in Figure 5; repeat. Sew D between two C-E units, again referring to Figure 5.

**Step 12.** Arrange units in rows referring to the block drawing for placement of units. Join rows to complete one block; repeat for 15 blocks.

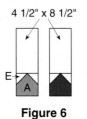

**Figure 4**
Complete 1 B-E
unit as shown.

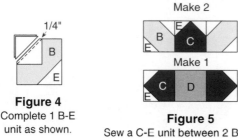

**Figure 5**
Sew a C-E unit between 2 B-E units.
Sew D between 2 C-E units.

**Step 13.** Sew a pink A-E unit to one end of a sashing segment as shown in Figure 6; repeat for six pink sashing strips. Repeat to make six purple sashing strips.

**Step 14.** Sew a sashing square between a pink A-E unit and a purple A-E unit as shown in Figure 7; repeat for 10 pink/purple sashing strips.

4 1/2" x 8 1/2"

**Figure 6**
Sew an A-E unit to 1 end
of a sashing segment.

**Figure 7**
Sew a sashing square
between 1 pink and 1
purple A-E unit.

**Step 15.** Join three blocks with a pink sashing strip and a purple sashing strip as shown in Figure 8; repeat for two rows.

**Figure 8**
Join 3 blocks with 1 pink
and 1 purple sashing strip.

**Step 16.** Join three blocks with two pink/purple sashing strips as shown in Figure 9; repeat for three rows.

Make 2

Make 1

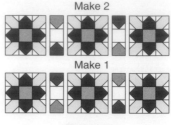

**Figure 9**
Join 3 blocks with 2 pink/purple
sashing strips.

**Step 17.** Sew a D square to opposite ends of a pink/purple sashing strip; sew a pink sashing strip and a purple sashing strip to each end as shown in Figure 10; repeat for four sashing rows.

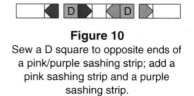

**Figure 10**
Sew a D square to opposite ends of
a pink/purple sashing strip; add a
pink sashing strip and a purple
sashing strip.

**Step 18.** Arrange block rows with sashing rows referring to the Placement Diagram for positioning of rows. Join rows to complete pieced center.

**Step 19.** Sew a 2 1/2" x 76 1/2" large pansy strip cut in Step 5 to opposite long sides of the pieced center; press seams toward strips. Sew a 2 1/2" x 48 1/2" strip to top and bottom; press seams toward strips.

**Step 20.** Join 20 C-E units to make a border strip referring to the Placement Diagram for positioning of units; repeat for two border strips. Sew a strip to opposite long sides of the pieced center.

**Step 21.** Join 12 C-E units to make a border strip; repeat for two border strips. Sew a D square to each end of each strip. Sew a strip to the top and bottom to complete the pieced top.

**Step 22.** Sandwich batting between the completed top and the prepared backing piece; pin or baste to hold. Quilt as desired by hand or machine. *Note: The sample shown was professionally machine-quilted.*

**Step 23.** Trim backing and batting even with top. Remove pins or basting.

**Step 24.** Bind with self-made or purchased binding to finish. ❧

# Tilted Star

By Judith Sandstrom

*Simple triangles and squares combine to make this child's star-design quilt.*

## Project Specifications

**Quilt Size:** 40" x 56"
**Block Size:** 8" x 8"
**Number of Blocks:** 24

## Materials

- 1/4 yard each pastel blue, lavender, green, pink and tan prints
- 5/8 yard navy solid
- 3/4 yard floral print
- 1 yard cream-on-cream print
- Batting 44" x 60"
- Backing 44" x 60"
- 5 3/4 yards self-made or purchased binding
- All-purpose thread to match fabrics
- Cream quilting thread
- Basic sewing supplies and tools, rotary cutter, mat and ruler

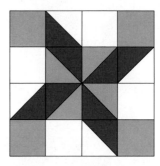

**Tilted Star**
8" x 8" Block

## Instructions

**Step 1.** Cut one strip tan print, six strips cream-on-cream print and two strips each pastel blue, lavender, green and pink prints 2 1/2"

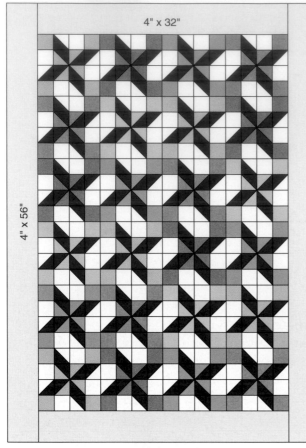

4" x 32"

4" x 56"

**Tilted Star**
Placement Diagram
40" x 56"

by fabric width; subcut strips into 2 1/2"
squares for A. You will need 16 tan print, 96
cream-on-cream print and 20 each pastel blue,
lavender, green and pink print A squares.

**Step 2.** Cut one strip tan print, four strips
cream-on-cream print, seven strips navy solid
and one strip each pastel blue, lavender, green
and pink prints 2 7/8" by fabric width; subcut all
strips into 2 7/8" square segments. Cut each segment in half on one diagonal to make B triangles. You will need 16 tan print, 96 cream-on-
cream print, 192 navy solid and 20 each pastel
blue, lavender, green and pink print B triangles.

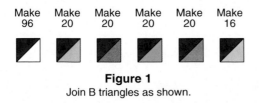

Make 96   Make 20   Make 20   Make 20   Make 20   Make 16

**Figure 1**
Join B triangles as shown.

**Step 3.** Referring to Figure 1, join B triangles in

the following color combinations:
cream/navy—96; blue/navy—20;
lavender/navy—20; green/navy—20;
pink/navy—20; and tan/navy—16.

**Step 4.** Arrange pieced B units with A squares
to make rows to complete blocks referring to
Figure 2 for positioning of pieces for each block
variation. Join units in rows; join rows to complete blocks. Make five each pastel blue, lavender, green and pink blocks and four tan blocks.

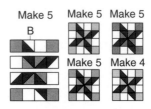

Make 5   Make 5   Make 5

Make 5   Make 4

**Figure 2**
Arrange B units with A to make
rows for each block; join rows
to complete 1 block.

**Step 5.** Referring to
Figure 3, arrange blocks
in six rows of four
blocks each; join blocks
in rows. Join rows to
complete the pieced
center; press seams in
one direction.

**Step 6.** Cut (and piece)
two strips each floral
print 4 1/2" x 32 1/2"
and 4 1/2" x 56 1/2".
Sew the shorter strips to
the top and bottom of
the pieced center; press
seams toward strips. Sew
the longer strips to opposite sides; press seams
toward strips.

Blue = 1
Lavender = 2
Green = 3
Pink = 4
Tan = 5

| 1 | 2 | 3 | 4 |
|---|---|---|---|
| 4 | 5 | 1 | 2 |
| 2 | 3 | 4 | 5 |
| 5 | 1 | 2 | 3 |
| 3 | 4 | 5 | 1 |
| 1 | 2 | 3 | 4 |

**Figure 3**
Arrange blocks in 6 rows of 4
blocks each referring to block
number for positioning.

**Step 7.** Sandwich batting between the completed top and the prepared backing piece; pin or
baste to hold. Quilt as desired. *Note: The sample shown was hand-quilted using cream quilting thread.*

**Step 8.** Trim backing and batting even with top.
Remove pins or basting.

**Step 9.** Bind with self-made or purchased binding to finish. ❧

# Clowning Around Kid's Quilt

By Janice Loewenthal

*Piecing and appliqué combine to make this colorful kid's quilt.*

## Project Specifications

**Quilt Size:** 50" x 50"

**Block Size:** 10" x 10"

**Number of Blocks:** 13

## Materials

- Scraps purple, red, green, yellow, lavender, white, black, brown and orange prints or solids
- 1/4 yard each green, blue and orange solids
- 3/8 yard red solid
- 1/2 yard yellow solid
- 1 yard blue print
- 1 1/4 yards blue multiplaid
- Batting 54" x 54"
- Backing 54" x 54"
- 6 yards self made or purchased binding
- All-purpose thread to match fabrics
- 3 yards fusible transfer web
- 2 1/2 yards fabric stabilizer
- Black 6-strand embroidery floss
- Basic sewing supplies and tools, rotary cutter, mat and ruler

**Sailor Clown**
10" x 10" Block

**Derby Clown**
10" x 10" Block

**Hatless Clown**
10" x 10" Block

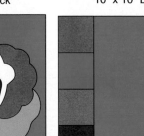

**Party Clown**
10" x 10" Block

**Top Hat Clown**
10" x 10" Block

**Split Bars Variation**
10" x 10" Block

## Instructions

### Making Clown Blocks

**Step 1.** Prepare templates for clown shapes using full-size patterns given.

**Step 2.** Trace shapes onto the paper side of the fusible transfer web as directed on each piece for number to cut. Cut out shapes, leaving a margin around each one.

**Step 3.** Fuse paper shapes to the wrong side of fabrics as directed on each piece for color. Cut out shapes on traced lines; remove paper backing.

**Step 4.** Cut five squares blue print 10 1/2" x 10 1/2". Lay clown drawing under one square, centering design. Trace lightly to transfer design; repeat for five different clown designs. *Note: The clown faces can be tilted differently on blocks and the arrangement of the facial features can vary in placement.*

**Clowning Around Kid's Quilt**
Placement Diagram
50" x 50"

**Step 5.** Lay pieces on each block in numerical order following pattern and marked lines. The hats are different on each clown; refer to the Placement Diagram for positioning of hats. *Note: Some hats are on top of the face while others are slipped underneath.* Refer to Figure 1 for numerical order placement for each design. Fuse shapes in place.

**Step 6.** Cut five squares fabric stabilizer 10" x 10". Place a square under each fused block.

**Step 7.** Using all-purpose thread to match fabrics, machine-appliqué each shape in place. Using black thread and a narrow satin stitch, stitch a mouth line in each mouth piece. When stitching is complete, remove stabilizer.

**Step 8.** Using 3 strands black embroidery floss, stitch eye shapes using pattern given on face shape.

### Making Split Bars Variation Blocks

**Step 1.** Cut two strips each red, blue, green and orange solids 3" by fabric width. Sew one strip of each color with right sides together along length in the color order given to make a strip set; repeat for two strip sets. Press seams in one direction.

**Step 2.** Cut each strip set into 3" segments as shown in Figure 2. You will need 16 segments.

**Step 3.** Cut eight rectangles blue print 5 1/2" x 10 1/2". Sew a pieced segment to each 10 1/2"

**Figure 1**
Arrange pieces in numerical order for each block as shown.

side of each rectangle referring to Figure 3 for placement of colors.

**Figure 2**
Cut each strip set
into 3" segments.

3"

**Step 4.** Prepare templates for star shapes using patterns given. Bond fusible transfer web to the wrong side of the yellow solid. Trace star shapes onto the paper side of the fused fabric referring to patterns for number to cut.

**Figure 3**
Sew a pieced segment to each
10 1/2" side of each rectangle.

**Step 5.** Cut out shapes on traced lines; remove paper backing.

**Step 6.** Fuse two small stars onto each Split Bars Variation block referring to the Placement Diagram and block drawing for positioning suggestions.

**Step 7.** Cut stabilizer squares to fit behind each star and pin in place. Using all-purpose thread to match fabric, machine-appliqué star shapes in place. When appliqué is complete, remove stabilizer.

**Completing Quilt**

**Step 1.** Join two Split Bars Variation blocks with one Clown block to make a row. *Note: Position Clown blocks as desired.* Join two Clown blocks with one Split Bars Variation block to make a row; repeat for two rows. Press seams in one direction.

**Step 2.** Join blocks in rows referring to the Placement Diagram; join rows to complete the pieced center. Press seams in one direction.

**Step 3.** Cut four strips blue multiplaid 10 1/2" x 30 1/2". Sew a strip to two opposite sides of the pieced center; press seams toward strips.

**Step 4.** Sew a Split Bars Variation block to each end of the remaining two strips as shown in Figure 4; press seams toward strips. Sew these strips to the top and bottom of the pieced center; press seams toward strips.

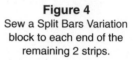

**Figure 4**
Sew a Split Bars Variation
block to each end of the
remaining 2 strips.

**Step 5.** Fuse two large stars onto each blue multiplaid border strip referring to the Placement Diagram for positioning suggestions.

**Step 6.** Machine-appliqué star shapes in place referring to Step 7 of Clown Blocks.

**Step 7.** Sandwich batting between the completed top and the prepared backing piece; pin or baste to hold. Quilt as desired. *Note: The sample shown was machine-quilted around clown shapes, 1/2" from star shapes and in the ditch of some block seams.*

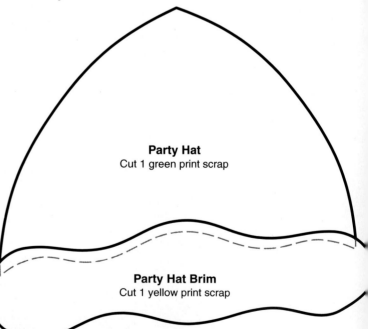

**Party Hat**
Cut 1 green print scrap

**Party Hat Brim**
Cut 1 yellow print scrap

**Step 8.** Trim backing and batting even with top. Remove pins or basting.

**Step 9.** Bind with self-made or purchased binding to finish. ❧

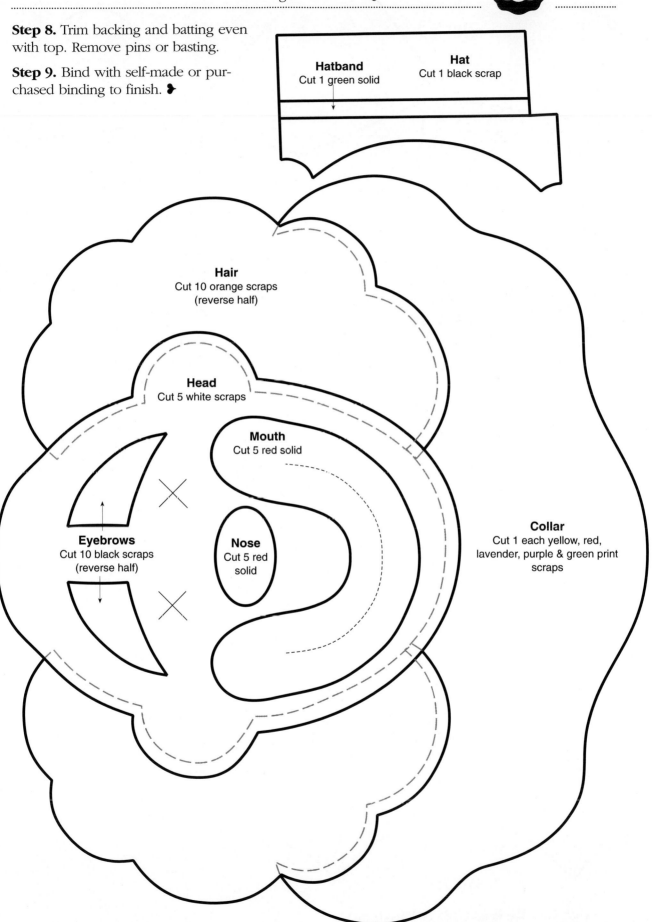

**Hatband**
Cut 1 green solid

**Hat**
Cut 1 black scrap

**Hair**
Cut 10 orange scraps
(reverse half)

**Head**
Cut 5 white scraps

**Mouth**
Cut 5 red solid

**Eyebrows**
Cut 10 black scraps
(reverse half)

**Nose**
Cut 5 red
solid

**Collar**
Cut 1 each yellow, red,
lavender, purple & green print
scraps

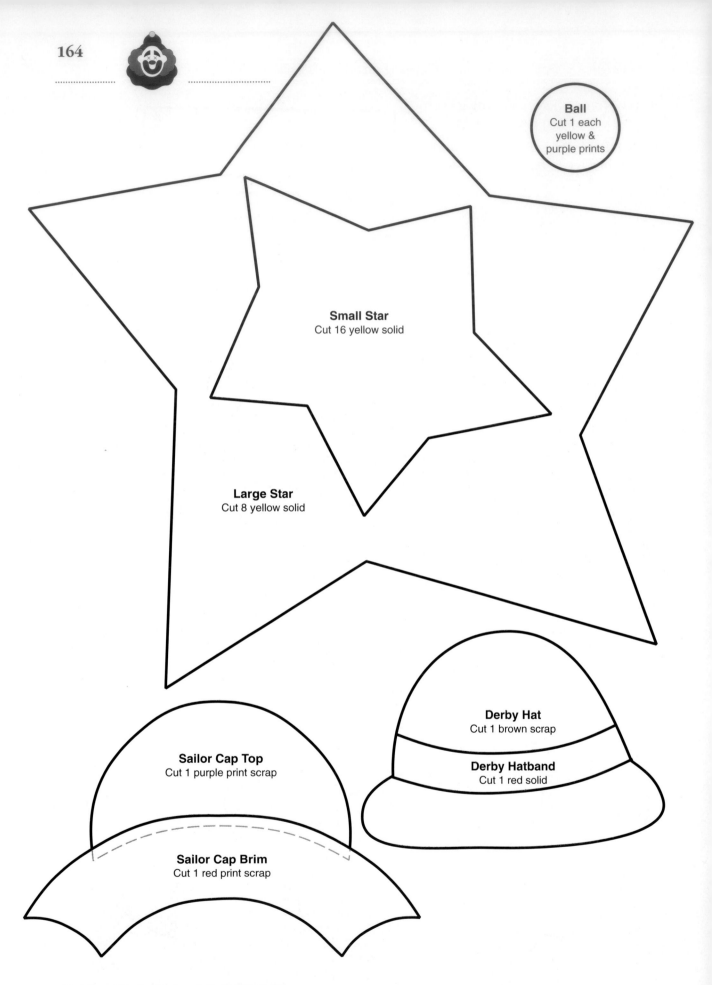

**Ball**
Cut 1 each
yellow &
purple prints

**Small Star**
Cut 16 yellow solid

**Large Star**
Cut 8 yellow solid

**Derby Hat**
Cut 1 brown scrap

**Derby Hatband**
Cut 1 red solid

**Sailor Cap Top**
Cut 1 purple print scrap

**Sailor Cap Brim**
Cut 1 red print scrap

# Quiltmaking Basics

## Materials & Supplies

### Fabrics

**Fabric Choices.** Quilts and quilted projects combine fabrics of many types, depending on the project. It is best to combine same-fiber-content fabrics when making quilted items.

**Buying Fabrics.** One hundred percent cotton fabrics are recommended for making quilts. Choose colors similar to those used in the quilts shown or colors of your own preference. Most quilt designs depend more on contrast of values than on the colors used to create the design.

**Preparing the Fabric for Use.** Fabrics may be prewashed or not, depending on your preference. Whether you do or don't, be sure your fabrics are colorfast and won't run onto each other when washed after use.

**Fabric Grain.** Fabrics are woven with threads going in a crosswise and lengthwise direction. The threads cross at right angles—the more threads per inch, the stronger the fabric.

The crosswise threads will stretch a little. The lengthwise threads will not stretch at all. Cutting the fabric at a 45-degree angle to the crosswise and lengthwise threads produces a bias edge which stretches a great deal when pulled (Figure 1).

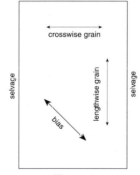

**Figure 1**
Drawing shows lengthwise, crosswise and bias threads.

If templates are given with patterns in this book, pay careful attention to the grain lines marked with arrows. These arrows indicate that the piece should be placed on the lengthwise grain with the arrow running on one thread. Although it is not necessary to examine the fabric and find a thread to match to, it is important to try to place the arrow with the lengthwise grain of the fabric (Figure 2).

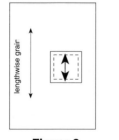

**Figure 2**
Place the template with marked arrow on the lengthwise grain of the fabric.

### Thread

For most piecing, good-quality cotton or cotton-covered polyester is the thread of choice. Inexpensive polyester threads are not recommended because they can cut the fibers of cotton fabrics.

Choose a color thread that will match or blend with the fabrics in your quilt. For projects pieced with dark and light color fabrics choose a neutral thread color, such as a medium gray, as a compromise between colors. Test by pulling at a stitched sample seam from the right side.

### Batting

Batting is the material used to give a quilt loft or thickness. It also adds warmth.

Batting size is listed in inches for each pattern to reflect the size needed to complete the quilt according to the instructions. Purchase the size large enough to cut the size you need for the quilt of your choice.

Some qualities to look for in batting are drapeability, resistance to fiber migration, loft and softness.

If you are unsure which kind of batting to use, purchase the smallest size batting available in the type you'd like to try. Test each sample on a small project. Choose the batting that you like working with most and that will result in the type of quilt you need.

### Tools & Equipment

There are few truly essential tools and little equipment required for quiltmaking. The basics include needles (hand-sewing and quilting betweens), pins (long, thin sharp pins are best), sharp scissors or shears, a thimble, template materials (plastic or cardboard), marking tools (chalk marker, water-erasable pen and a No. 2 pencil are a few) and a quilting frame or hoop. For piecing and/or quilting by machine, add a sewing machine to the list.

Other necessary sewing basics are a seam ripper, pincushion, measuring tape and an iron. For choosing colors or quilting designs for your quilt, or for designing your own quilt, it is helpful to have graph paper, tracing paper, colored pencils or markers and a ruler on hand.

For making strip-pieced quilts, a rotary cutter, mat and specialty rulers are often used. We recommend an ergonomic rotary cutter, a large self-healing mat and several rulers. If you can choose only one size, a 6" x 24" marked in 1/8" or 1/4" increments is recommended.

## Construction Methods

### Templates

**Traditional Templates.** While many quilt instructions in this book use rotary-cut strips and quick-sewing methods, a few patterns require templates. Templates are like the pattern pieces used to sew a garment. They are used to cut the fabric pieces which make up the quilt top. There are two types—templates that include a 1/4" seam allowance and those that don't.

Choose the template material and the pattern.

**Figure 3**
Mark each template with the pattern name and piece identification.

**Figure 4**
This pattern uses reversed pieces.

Transfer the pattern shapes to the template material with a sharp No. 2 lead pencil. Write the pattern name, piece letter or number, grain line and number to cut for one block or whole quilt on each piece as shown in Figure 3.

Some patterns require a reversed piece (Figure 4). These patterns are labeled with an R after the piece letter; for example, A and AR. To reverse a template, first cut it with the labeled side up and then with the labeled side down. Compare these to the right and left fronts of a blouse. When making a garment, you accomplish reversed pieces when cutting the pattern on two layers of fabric placed with right sides together. This can be done when cutting templates as well.

If cutting one layer of fabric at a time, first trace the template onto the backside of the fabric with the marked side down; turn the template over with the marked side up to make reverse pieces.

Appliqué patterns given in this book do not include a seam allowance. Most designs are given in one drawing rather than individual pieces. This saves space while giving you the complete design to trace on the background block to help with placement of the pieces later. Make templates for each shape using the drawing for exact size. Remember to label each piece as for piecing templates.

For hand appliqué, add a seam allowance when cutting pieces from fabric. You may trace the template with label side up on the right side of the fabric if you are careful to mark lightly. The traced line is then the guide for turning the edges under when stitching.

If you prefer to mark on the wrong side of the fabric, turn the template over if you want the pattern to face the same way it does on the page.

For machine appliqué, a seam allowance is not necessary. Trace template onto the right side of the fabric with label facing up. Cut around shape on the traced line.

# Piecing

**Hand-Piecing Basics.** When hand-piecing it is easier to begin with templates which do not include the 1/4" seam allowance. Place the template on the wrong side of the fabric, lining up the marked grain line with lengthwise or crosswise fabric grain. If the piece does not have to be reversed, place with labeled side up. Trace around shape; move, leaving 1/2" between the shapes, and mark again.

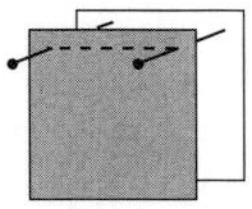

**Figure 5**
Stick a pin through fabrics to match the beginning of the seam.

When you have marked the appropriate number of pieces, cut out pieces, leaving 1/4" beyond marked line all around each piece.

To piece, refer to assembly drawings to piece units and blocks, if provided. To join two units, place the patches with right sides together. Stick a pin in at the beginning of the seam through both fabric patches, matching the beginning points (Figure 5); for hand-piecing, the seam begins on the traced line, not at the edge of the fabric (see Figure 6).

**Figure 6**
Begin hand-piecing at seam, not at the edge of the fabric. Continue stitching along seam line.

Thread a sharp needle; knot one strand of the thread at the end. Remove the pin and insert the needle in the hole; make a short stitch and then a backstitch right over the first stitch.

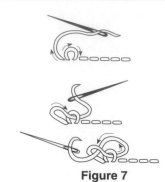

**Figure 7**
Make a loop in a backstitch to make a knot.

Continue making short stitches with several stitches on the needle at one time. As you stitch, check the back piece often to assure accurate stitching on the seam line. Take a stitch at the end of the seam; backstitch and knot at the same time as shown in Figure 7.

Seams on hand-pieced fabric patches may be finger-pressed toward the darker fabric.

To sew units together, pin fabric patches together, matching seams. Sew as above except where seams meet; at these intersections, backstitch, go through seam to next piece and backstitch again to secure seam joint.

Not all pieced blocks can be stitched with straight seams or in rows. Some patterns require set-in pieces. To begin a set-in seam on a star pattern, pin one side of the square to the proper side of the star point with right sides together, matching corners. Start stitching at the seam line on the outside point; stitch on the marked seam line to the end of the seam line at the center referring to Figure 8.

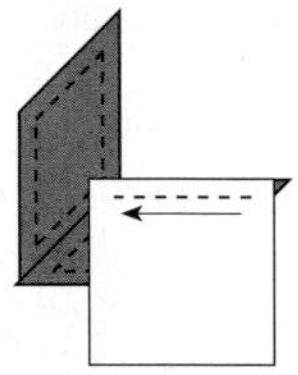

**Figure 8**
To set a square into a diamond point, match seams and stitch from outside edge to center.

Bring around the adjacent side and pin to the next star point, matching seams. Continue the stitching line from the adjacent seam through corners and to the outside edge of the square as shown in Figure 9.

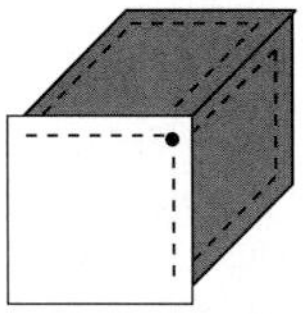

**Figure 9**
Continue stitching the adjacent side of the square to the next diamond shape in 1 seam from center to outside as shown.

**Machine-Piecing.**
If making templates, include the 1/4" seam allowance on the template for machine-piecing. Place template on the wrong side of the fabric as for hand-piecing except butt pieces against one another when tracing.

Set machine on 2.5 or 12–15 stitches per inch. Join pieces as for hand-piecing for set-in seams; but for other straight seams, begin and end sewing at the end of the fabric patch sewn as shown in Figure 10. No backstitching is

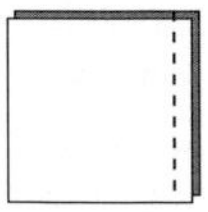

**Figure 10**
Begin machine-piecing at the end of the piece, not at the end of the seam.

necessary when machine-stitching.

Join units as for hand-piecing referring to the piecing diagrams where needed. Chain piecing (Figure 11—sewing several like units before sewing other units) saves time by eliminating beginning and ending stitches.

When joining machine-pieced units, match seams against each other with seam allowances pressed in opposite directions to reduce bulk and make perfect matching of seams possible (Figure 12).

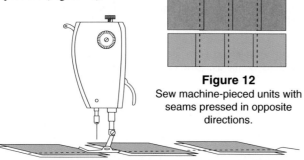

**Figure 12**
Sew machine-pieced units with seams pressed in opposite directions.

**Figure 11**
Units may be chain-pieced to save time.

# Cutting

**Quick-Cutting.**
Quick-cutting and piecing strips are recommended for making many of the projects in this book. Templates are completely eliminated; instead, a rotary cutter, plastic ruler and mat are used to cut fabric pieces.

**Figure 13**
Fold fabric and straighten as shown.

**Figure 14**
Wavy strips result if fabric is not straightened before cutting.

When rotary-cutting strips, straighten raw edges of fabric by folding fabric in fourths across the width as shown in Figure 13. Press down flat; place ruler on fabric square with edge of fabric and make one cut from the folded edge to the outside edge. If strips are not straightened, a wavy strip will result as shown in Figure 14.

Always cut away from your body, holding the ruler firmly with the non-cutting hand. Keep fingers away from the edge of the ruler as it is easy for the rotary cutter to slip and jump over the edge of the ruler if cutting is not properly done.

For many strip-pieced blocks two strips are stitched together as shown in Figure 15. The strips are stitched, pressed and cut into segments as shown in Figure 16.

**Figure 15**
Join 2 strips as shown.

The cut segments are arranged as shown in Figure 17 and stitched to complete, in this example, one Four-

**Figure 16**
Cut segments from the stitched strip set.

Patch block. Although the block shown is very simple, the same methods may be used for more complicated patterns.

The direction to press seams on strip sets is important for accurate piecing later. The normal rule for pressing is to press seams toward the darker fabric to keep the colors from showing through on lighter colors later. For joining segments from strip sets, this rule doesn't always apply.

It is best if seams on adjacent rows are pressed in opposite directions. When aligning segments to stitch rows together, if pressed properly, seam joints will have a seam going in both directions as shown in Figure 18.

If a square is required for the pattern, it can be subcut from a strip as shown in Figure 19.

If you need right triangles with the straight grain on the short sides, you can use the same method, but you need to figure out how wide to cut the strip. Measure the finished size of one short side of the triangle. Add 7/8" to this size for seam allowance. Cut fabric strips this width; cut the strips into the same increment to create squares. Cut the squares on the diagonal to produce triangles. For example, if you need a triangle with a 2" finished height, cut the strips 2 7/8" by the width of the fabric. Cut the strips into 2 7/8" squares. Cut each square on the diagonal to produce the correct-size triangle with the grain on the short sides (Figure 20).

Triangles sewn together to make squares are called half-square triangles or triangle/squares. When joined, the triangle/square unit has the straight of grain on all outside edges of the block.

Another method of making triangle/squares is shown in Figure 21. Layer two squares with right sides together; draw a diagonal line through the center. Stitch 1/4" on both sides of the line. Cut apart on the drawn line to reveal two stitched triangle/squares.

If you need triangles with the straight of grain on the diagonal, such as for fill-in triangles on the outside edges of a diagonal-set quilt, the procedure is a bit different.

To make these triangles, a square is cut on both diagonals; thus, the straight of grain is on the longest or diagonal side

**Figure 17**
Arrange cut segments to make a Four-Patch block.

**Figure 18**
Seams go in both directions at seam joints.

**Figure 19**
Fold binding at a 45-degree angle up and away from quilt as shown.

**Figure 20**
Cut 2" (finished size) triangles from 2 7/8" squares as shown.

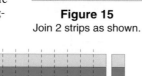

**Figure 21**
Mark a diagonal line on the square; stitch 1/4" on each side of the line. Cut on line to reveal stitched triangle/squares.

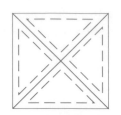

(Figure 22). To figure out the size to cut the square, add 1 1/4" to the needed finished size of the longest side of the triangle. For example, if you need a triangle with a 12" finished diagonal, cut a 13 1/4" square.

If templates are given, use their measurements to cut fabric strips to correspond with that measurement. The template may be used on the strip to cut pieces quickly. Strip cutting works best for squares, triangles, rectangles and diamonds. Odd-shaped templates are difficult to cut in multiple layers using a rotary cutter.

**Figure 22**
Add 1 1/4" to the finished size of the longest side of the triangle needed and cut on both diagonals to make a quarter-square triangle.

# Foundation Piecing

**Foundation Piecing.** Paper or fabric foundation pieces are used to make very accurate blocks, provide stability for weak fabrics, and add body and weight to the finished quilt.

Temporary foundation materials include paper, tracing paper, freezer paper and removable interfacing. Permanent foundations include utility fabrics, nonwoven interfacing, flannel, fleece and batting.

Methods of marking foundations include basting lines, pencils or pens, needle punching, tracing wheel, hot-iron transfers, copy machine, premarked, stamps or stencils.

There are two methods of foundation piecing—under-piecing and top-piecing. When under-piecing, the pattern is reversed when tracing. We have not included any patterns for top-piecing. *Note: All patterns for which we recommend paper piecing are already reversed in full-size drawings given.*

To under-piece, place a scrap of fabric larger than the lined space on the unlined side of the paper in the No. 1 position. Place piece 2 right sides together with piece 1; pin on seam line, and fold back to check that the piece will cover space 2 before stitching.

Stitch along line on the lined side of the paper—fabric will not be visible. Sew several stitches beyond the beginning and ending of the line. Backstitching is not required as another fabric seam will cover this seam.

Remove pin; finger-press piece 2 flat. Continue adding all pieces in numerical order in the same manner until all pieces are stitched to paper. Trim excess to outside line (1/4" larger all around than finished size of the block).

Tracing paper can be used as a temporary foundation. It is removed when blocks are complete and stitched together. To paper-piece, copy patterns using a copy machine or trace each block individually. Measure the finished paper foundations to insure accuracy in copying.

## Tips & Techniques

If you cannot see the lines on the backside of the paper when paper-piecing, draw over lines with a small felt-tip marker. The lines should now be visible on the backside to help with placement of fabric pieces.

# Appliqué

Appliqué is the process of applying one piece of fabric on top of another for decorative or functional purposes.

**Making Templates.** Most appliqué designs given here are shown as full-size drawings for the completed designs. The drawings show dotted lines to indicate where one piece overlaps another. Other marks indicate placement of embroidery stitches for decorative purposes such as eyes, lips, flowers, etc.

For hand appliqué, trace each template onto the right side of the fabric with template right side up. Cut around shape, adding a 1/8"–1/4" seam allowance.

Before the actual appliqué process begins, cut the background block and prepare it for stitching. Most appliqué designs are centered on the block. To find the center of the background square, fold it in half and in half again; crease with your fingers. Now unfold and fold diagonally and crease; repeat for other corners referring to Figure 23. Center-line creases help position the design. If centering the appliqué design is important, an

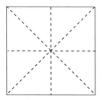

**Figure 23**
Fold background to mark centers as shown.

X has been placed on each drawing to mark the center of the design. Match the X with the creased center of the background block when placing pieces.

If you have a full-size drawing of the design, as is given with most appliqué designs in this book, it might help you to draw on the background block to help with placement. Transfer the design to a large piece of tracing paper. Place the paper on top of the design; use masking tape to hold in place. Trace design onto paper.

If you don't have a light box, tape the pattern on a window; center the background block on top and tape in place. Trace the design onto the background block with a water-erasable marker or chalk pencil. This drawing will mark exactly where the fabric pieces should be placed on the background block.

**Hand Appliqué.** Traditional hand appliqué uses a template made from the desired finished shape without seam allowance added.

After fabric is prepared, trace the desired shape onto the right side of the fabric with a water-erasable marker, light lead or chalk pencil. Leave at least 1/2" between design motifs when tracing to allow for the seam allowance when cutting out the shapes.

When the desired number of shapes needed has been drawn on the fabric pieces, cut out shapes leaving 1/8"–1/4" all around drawn line for turning under.

Turn the shape's edges over on the drawn or stitched line. When turning the edges under, make sharp corners sharp and smooth edges smooth. The fabric patch should retain the shape of the template used to cut it.

When turning in concave curves, clip to seams and

**Figure 24**
Concave curves should be clipped before turning as shown.

baste the seam allowance over as shown in Figure 24.

During the actual appliqué process, you may be layering one shape on top of another. Where two fabrics overlap, the underneath piece does not have to be turned under or stitched down.

If possible, trim away the underneath fabric when the block is finished by carefully cutting away the background from underneath and then cutting away unnecessary layers to reduce bulk and avoid shadows from darker fabrics showing through on light fabrics.

For hand appliqué, position the fabric shapes on the background block and pin or baste them in place. Using a blind stitch or appliqué stitch, sew pieces in place with matching thread and small stitches. Start with background pieces first and work up to foreground pieces. Appliqué the pieces in place on the background in numerical order, if given, layering as necessary.

**Machine Appliqué.** There are several products available to help make the machine-appliqué process easier and faster.

Fusible transfer web is a commercial product similar to iron-on interfacings except it has two sticky sides. It is used to adhere appliqué shapes to the background with heat. Paper is adhered to one side of the web.

To use, dry-iron the sticky side of the fusible product onto the wrong side of the chosen fabric. Draw desired shapes onto the paper and cut them out. Peel off the paper and dry-iron the shapes in place on the background fabric. The shape will stay in place while you stitch around it. This process adds a little bulk or stiffness to the appliquéd shape and

makes hand quilting through the layers difficult.

For successful machine appliqué a tear-off stabilizer is recommended. This product is placed under the background fabric while machine appliqué is being done. It is torn away when the work is finished. This kind of stabilizer keeps the background fabric from pulling during the machine-appliqué process.

During the actual machine-appliqué process, you will be layering one shape on top of another. Where two fabrics overlap, the underneath piece does not have to be turned under or stitched down.

Thread the top of the machine with thread to match the fabric patches or with threads that coordinate or contrast with fabrics. Rayon thread is a good choice when a sheen is desired on the finished appliqué stitches. Do not use rayon thread in the bobbin; use all-purpose thread.

Set your machine to make a zigzag stitch and practice on scraps of similar weight to check the tension. If you can see the bobbin thread on the top of the appliqué, adjust your machine to make a balanced stitch. Different-width stitches are available; choose one that will not overpower the appliqué shapes. In some cases these appliqué stitches will be used as decorative stitches as well and you may want the thread to show.

If using a stabilizer, place this under the background fabric and pin or fuse in place. Place shapes as for hand-appliqué and stitch all around shapes by machine.

When all machine work is complete, remove stabilizer from the back referring to the manufacturer's instructions.

# Transferring Embroidery Designs

When transferring embroidery designs to a background fabric, fold the background fabric to find the center; crease to mark. Find the center of the embroidery design, if not marked, by folding and creasing in the same manner.

If you do not have a light box as a light source, tape the transfer design to a window. Center the background piece over the center of the design; tape in place.

Use a water-erasable marker or pencil to trace the lines from the pattern onto the background. If the project will be stitched over a long period of time, a light pencil might make a better choice as water-erasable markers do disappear with humidity.

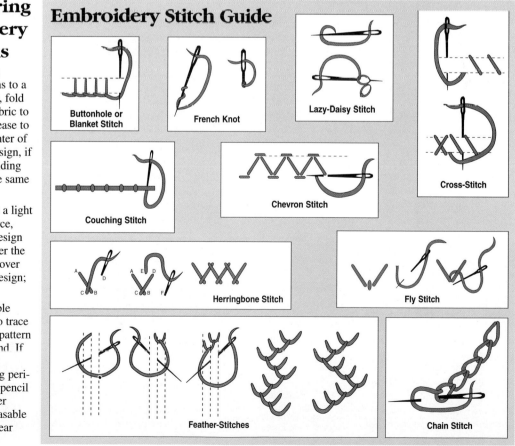

**Embroidery Stitch Guide**

Buttonhole or Blanket Stitch

French Knot

Lazy-Daisy Stitch

Cross-Stitch

Couching Stitch

Chevron Stitch

Herringbone Stitch

Fly Stitch

Feather-Stitches

Chain Stitch

# Putting It All Together

Many steps are required to prepare a quilt top for quilting, including setting the blocks together, adding borders, choosing and marking quilting designs, layering the top, batting and backing for quilting, quilting or tying the layers and finishing the edges of the quilt.

As you begin the process of finishing your quilt top, strive for a neat, flat quilt with square sides and corners, not for perfection—that will come with time and practice.

## Finishing the Top

**Settings.** Most quilts are made by sewing individual blocks together in rows which, when joined, create a design. There are several other methods used to join blocks. Sometimes the setting choice is determined by the block's design. For example, a house block should be placed upright on a quilt, not sideways or upside down.

Plain blocks can be alternated with pieced or appliquéd blocks in a straight set. Making a quilt using plain blocks saves time; half the number of pieced or appliquéd blocks are needed to make the same-size quilt as shown in Figure 1.

**Adding Borders.** Borders are an integral part of the quilt and should complement the colors and designs used in the quilt center. Borders frame a quilt just like a mat and frame do a picture.

If fabric strips are added for borders, they may be mitered or butted at the corners as shown in Figures 2 and 3.

To determine the size for butted-border strips, measure across the center of the completed quilt top from one side raw edge to the other side raw edge. This measurement will include a 1/4" seam allowance. Cut two border strips that length by the chosen width of the border. Sew these strips to the top and bottom of the pieced center referring to Figure 4. Press the seam allowance toward the border strips.

Measure across the completed quilt top at the center, from top raw edge to bottom raw edge,

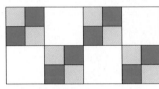

**Figure 1**
Alternate plain blocks with pieced block to save time.

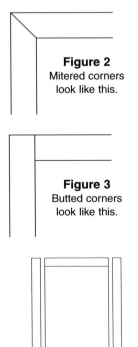

**Figure 2**
Mitered corners look like this.

**Figure 3**
Butted corners look like this.

**Figure 4**
Sew border strips to opposite sides; sew remaining 2 strips to remaining sides to make butted corners.

including the two border strips already added. Cut two border strips that length by the chosen width of the border. Sew a strip to each of the two remaining sides as shown in Figure 4. Press the seams toward the border strips.

To make mitered corners, measure the quilt as before. To this add twice the width of the border and 1/2" for seam allowances to determine the length of the strips. Repeat for opposite sides. Center and sew on each strip, stopping stitching 1/4" from corner, leaving the remainder of the strip dangling.

Press corners at a 45-degree angle to form a crease. Stitch from the inside quilt corner to the outside on the creased line. Trim excess away after stitching and press mitered seams open (Figures 5–7).

Carefully press the entire quilt top. Avoid pulling and stretching while pressing, which would distort shapes.

**Figure 5**
For mitered corner, stitch strip, stopping 1/4" from corner seam.

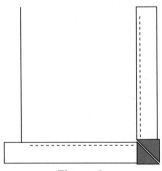

**Figure 6**
Fold and press corner to make a 45-degree angle.

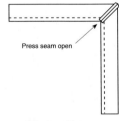

Press seam open

**Figure 7**
Trim away excess from underneath when stitching is complete. Press seams open.

## Getting Ready to Quilt

**Choosing a Quilting Design.** If you choose to hand- or machine-quilt your finished top, you will need to choose a design for quilting.

There are several types of quilting designs, some of which may not have to be marked. The easiest of the unmarked designs is in-the-ditch quilting. Here the quilting stitches are placed in the valley created by the seams joining two pieces together or next to the edge of an appliqué design. There is no need to mark a top for in-the-ditch quilting. Machine quilters choose this option because the stitches are not as obvious on the finished quilt (Figure 8).

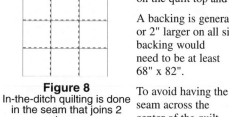

**Figure 8**
In-the-ditch quilting is done in the seam that joins 2 pieces.

Outline-quilting 1/4" or more away from seams or appliqué shapes is another no-mark alternative (Figure 9) which prevents having to sew through the layers made by seams, thus making stitching easier.

**Figure 9**
Outline-quilting 1/4" away from seam is a popular choice for quilting.

If you are not comfortable eyeballing the 1/4" (or other distance), masking tape is available in different widths and is helpful to place on straight-edge designs to mark the quilting line. If using masking tape, place the tape right up against the seam and quilt close to the other edge.

**Figure 10**
Machine meander quilting fills in large spaces.

Meander or free-motion quilting by machine fills in open spaces and doesn't require marking. It is fun and easy to stitch as shown in Figure 10.

**Marking the Top for Quilting or Tying.** If you choose a fancy or all-over design for quilting, you will need to transfer the design to your quilt top before layering with the backing and batting. You may use a sharp medium-lead or silver pencil on light background fabrics. Test the pencil marks to guarantee that they will wash out of your quilt top when quilting is complete; or be sure your quilting stitches cover the pencil marks. Mechanical pencils with very fine points may be used successfully to mark quilts.

Manufactured quilt-design templates are available in many designs and sizes and are cut out of a durable plastic template material which is easy to use.

To make a permanent quilt-design template, choose a template material on which to transfer the design. See-through plastic is the best as it will let you place the design while allowing you to see where it is in relation to your quilt design without moving it. Place the design on the quilt top where you want it and trace around it with your marking tool. Pick up the quilting template and place again; repeat marking.

No matter what marking method you use, remember—the marked lines should never show on the finished quilt. When the top is marked, it is ready for layering.

**Preparing the Quilt Backing.** The quilt backing is a very important feature of your quilt. In most cases, the materials list for each quilt in this book gives the size requirements for the backing, not the yardage needed. Exceptions to this are when the backing fabric is also used on the quilt top and yardage is given for that fabric.

A backing is generally cut at least 4" larger than the quilt top or 2" larger on all sides. For a 64" x 78" finished quilt, the backing would need to be at least 68" x 82".

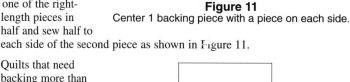

**Figure 11**
Center 1 backing piece with a piece on each side.

To avoid having the seam across the center of the quilt backing, cut or tear one of the right-length pieces in half and sew half to each side of the second piece as shown in Figure 11.

Quilts that need backing more than 88" wide may be pieced in horizontal pieces as shown in Figure 12.

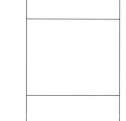

**Figure 12**
Horizontal seams may be used on backing pieces.

**Layering the Quilt Sandwich.** Layering the quilt top with the batting and backing is time-consuming. Open the batting several days before you need it and place over a bed or flat on the floor to help flatten the creases caused from its being folded up in the bag for so long.

Iron the backing piece, folding in half both vertically and horizontally and pressing to mark centers.

If you will not be quilting on a frame, place the backing right side down on a clean floor or table. Start in the center and push any wrinkles or bunches flat. Use masking tape to tape the edges to the floor or large clips to hold the backing to the edges of the table. The backing should be taut.

Place the batting on top of the backing, matching centers using fold lines as guides; flatten out any wrinkles. Trim the batting to the same size as the backing.

Fold the quilt top in half lengthwise and place on top of the batting, wrong side against the batting, matching centers. Unfold quilt and, working from the center to the outside edges, smooth out any wrinkles or lumps.

To hold the quilt layers together for quilting, baste by hand or use safety pins. If basting by hand, thread a long thin needle with a long piece of unknotted white or off-white thread. Starting in the center and leaving a long tail, make 4"–6" stitches toward the outside edge of the quilt top, smoothing as you baste. Start at the center again and work toward the outside as shown in Figure 13.

**Figure 13**
Baste from the center to the outside edges.

If quilting by machine, you may prefer to use safety pins for holding your quilt sandwich together. Start in the center of the quilt and pin to the outside, leaving pins open until all are placed. When you are satisfied that all layers are smooth, close the pins.

# Quilting

**Hand Quilting.** Hand quilting is the process of placing stitches through the quilt top, batting and backing to hold them together. While it is a functional process, it also adds beauty and loft to the finished quilt.

To begin, thread a sharp between needle with an 18" piece of quilting thread. Tie a small knot in the end of the thread. Position the needle about 1/2" to 1" away from the starting

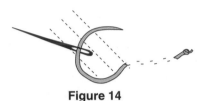

**Figure 14**
Start the needle through the top layer of fabric 1/2"–1" away from quilting line with knot on top of fabric.

point on quilt top. Sink the needle through the top into the batting layer but not through the backing. Pull the needle up at the starting point of the quilting design. Pull the needle and thread until the knot sinks through the top into the batting (Figure 14).

Some stitchers like to take a backstitch at the beginning while others prefer to begin the first stitch here. Take small, even running stitches along the marked quilting line (Figure 15). Keep one hand positioned underneath to feel the needle go all the way through to the backing.

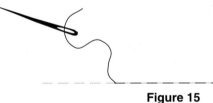

**Figure 15**
Make small, even running stitches on marked quilting line.

**Machine Quilting.** Successful machine quilting requires practice and a good relationship with your sewing machine.

Prepare the quilt for machine quilting in the same way as for hand quilting. Use safety pins to hold the layers together instead of basting with thread.

Presser-foot quilting is best used for straight-line quilting because the presser bar lever does not need to be continually lifted.

Set the machine on a longer stitch length (3 or eight to 10 stitches to the inch). Too tight a stitch causes puckering and fabric tucks, either on the quilt top or backing. An even-feed or walking foot helps to eliminate the tucks and puckering by feeding the upper and lower layers through the machine evenly. Before you begin, loosen the amount of pressure on the presser foot.

Special machine-quilting needles work best to penetrate the three layers in your quilt.

Decide on a design. Quilting in the ditch is not quite as visible, but if you quilt with the feed dogs engaged, it means turning the quilt frequently. It is not easy to fit a rolled-up quilt through the small opening on the sewing machine head.

Meander quilting is the easiest way to machine-quilt—and it is fun. Meander quilting is done using an appliqué or darning foot with the feed dogs dropped. It is sort of like scribbling. Simply move the quilt top around under the foot and make stitches in a random pattern to fill the space. The same method may be used to outline a quilt design. The trick is the same as in hand-quilting; you are striving for stitches of uniform size. Your hands are in complete control of the design.

If machine-quilting is of interest to you, there are several very good books available at quilt shops that will help you become a successful machine quilter.

**Tied Quilts, or Comforters.** Would you rather tie your quilt layers together than quilt them? Tied quilts are often referred to as comforters. The advantage of tying is that it takes so much less time and the required skills can be learned quickly.

If a top will be tied, choose a thick, bonded batting—one that will not separate during washing. For tying, use pearl cotton, embroidery floss, or strong yarn in colors that match or coordinate with the fabrics in your quilt top.

Decide on a pattern for tying. Many quilts are tied at the corners and centers of the blocks and at sashing joints. Try to tie every 4"–6". Special designs can be used for tying, but most quilts are tied in conventional ways. Begin tying in the center and work to the outside edges.

To make the tie, thread a large needle with a long thread (yarn, floss or crochet cotton); do not knot. Push the needle through the quilt top to the back, leaving a 3"–4" length on top. Move the needle to the next position without cutting thread. Take another stitch through the layers; repeat until thread is almost used up.

Cut thread between stitches, leaving an equal amount of thread on each stitch. Tie a knot with the two thread ends. Tie again to make a square knot referring to Figure 16. Trim thread ends to desired length.

**Figure 16**
Make a square knot as shown.

## Finishing the Edges

After your quilt is tied or quilted, the edges need to be finished. Decide how you want the edges of your quilt finished before layering the backing and batting with the quilt top.

**Without Binding—Self-Finish.** There is one way to eliminate adding an edge finish. This is done before quilting. Place the batting on a flat surface. Place the pieced top right side up on the batting. Place the backing right sides together with the pieced top. Pin and/or baste the layers together to hold flat referring to page 171.

Begin stitching in the center of one side using a 1/4" seam allowance, reversing at the beginning and end of the seam. Continue stitching all around and back to the beginning side. Leave a 12" or larger opening. Clip corners to reduce excess. Turn right side out through the opening. Slipstitch the opening closed by hand. The quilt may now be quilted by hand or machine.

The disadvantage to this method is that once the edges are sewn in, any creases or wrinkles that might form during the quilting process cannot be flattened out. Tying is the preferred method for finishing a quilt constructed using this method.

Bringing the backing fabric to the front is another way to finish the quilt's edge without binding. To accomplish this, complete the quilt as for hand or machine quilting. Trim the batting *only* even with the front. Trim the backing 1" larger than the completed top all around.

Turn the backing edge in 1/2" and then turn over to the front along edge of batting. The folded edge may be machine-stitched close to the edge through all layers, or blind-stitched in place to finish.

The front may be turned to the back. If using this method, a wider front border is needed. The backing and batting are trimmed 1" smaller than the top and the top edge is turned under 1/2" and then turned to the back and stitched in place.

One more method of self-finish may be used. The top and backing may be stitched together by hand at the edge. To accomplish this, all quilting must be stopped 1/2" from the quilt-top edge. The top and backing of the quilt are trimmed even and the batting is trimmed to 1/4"–1/2" smaller. The edges of the top and backing are turned in 1/4"–1/2" and blind-stitched together at the very edge.

These methods do not require the use of extra fabric and save time in preparation of binding strips; they are not as durable as an added binding.

**Binding.** The technique of adding extra fabric at the edges of the quilt is called binding. The binding encloses the edges and adds an extra layer of fabric for durability.

To prepare the quilt for the addition of the binding, trim the batting and backing layers flush with the top of the quilt using a rotary cutter and ruler or shears. Using a walking-foot attachment (sometimes called an even-feed foot attachment), machine-baste the three layers together all around approximately 1/8" from the cut edge.

The list of materials given with each quilt in this book often includes a number of yards of self-made or purchased binding. Bias binding may be purchased in packages and in many colors. The advantage to self-made binding is that you can use fabrics from your quilt to coordinate colors.

Double-fold, straight-grain binding and double-fold, bias-grain binding are two of the most commonly used types of binding.

Double-fold, straight-grain binding is used on smaller projects with right-angle corners. Double-fold, bias-grain binding is best suited for bed-size quilts or quilts with rounded corners.

To make double-fold, straight-grain binding, cut 2"-wide strips of fabric across the width or down the length of the fabric totaling the perimeter of the quilt plus 10". The strips are joined as shown in Figure 17 and pressed in half wrong sides together along the length using an iron on a cotton setting with no steam.

**Figure 17**
Join binding strips in a diagonal seam to eliminate bulk as shown.

Lining up the raw edges, place the binding on the top of the quilt and begin sewing (again using the walking foot) approximately 6" from the beginning of the binding strip. Stop sewing 1/4" from the first corner, leave the needle in the quilt, turn and sew diagonally to the corner as shown in Figure 18.

**Figure 18**
Sew to within 1/4" of corner; leave needle in quilt, turn and stitch diagonally off the corner of the quilt.

Fold the binding at a 45-degree angle up and away from the quilt as shown in Figure 19 and back down flush with the raw edges. Starting at the top raw edge of the quilt, begin sewing the next side as shown in Figure 20. Repeat at the next three corners.

As you approach the beginning of the binding strip, stop stitching and overlap the binding 1/2" from the edge; trim. Join the two ends with a 1/4" seam allowance and press the seam open. Reposition the joined binding along the edge of the quilt and resume stitching to the beginning.

**Figure 19**
Fold binding at a 45-degree angle up and away from quilt as shown.

To finish, bring the folded edge of the binding over the raw edges and blind-stitch the binding in place over the machine-stitching line on the backside. Hand-miter the corners on the back as shown in Figure 21.

If you are making a quilt to be used on a bed, you will want to use double-fold, bias-grain bindings because the many threads that cross each other along the fold at the edge of the quilt make it a more durable binding.

**Figure 20**
Fold the binding strips back down, flush with the raw edge, and begin sewing.

Cut 2"-wide bias strips from a large square of fabric. Join the strips as illustrated in Figure 17 and press the seams open. Fold the beginning end of the bias strip 1/4" from the raw edge and press. Fold the joined strips in half along

**Figure 21**
Miter and stitch the corners as shown.

**Figure 22**
Fold end in and press strip in half.

the long side, wrong sides together, and press with no steam (Figure 22).

Follow the same procedures as previously described for preparing the quilt top and sewing the binding to the quilt top. Treat the corners just as you treated them with straight-grain binding.

Since you are using bias-grain binding, you do have the option to just eliminate the corners if this option doesn't interfere with the patchwork in the quilt. Round the corners off by placing one of your dinner plates at the corner and rotary-cutting the gentle curve (Figure 23).

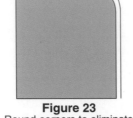

**Figure 23**
Round corners to eliminate square-corner finishes.

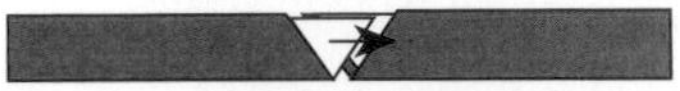

As you approach the beginning of the binding strip, stop stitching and lay the end across the beginning so it will slip inside the fold. Cut the end at a 45-degree angle so the raw edges are contained inside the beginning of the strip (Figure 24). Resume stitching to the beginning. Bring the fold to the back of the quilt and hand-stitch as previously described.

**Figure 24**
End the binding strips as shown.

Overlapped corners are not quite as easy as rounded ones, but a bit easier than mitering. To make overlapped corners, sew binding strips to opposite sides of the quilt top. Stitch edges down to finish. Trim ends even.

Sew a strip to each remaining side, leaving 1 1/2"–2" excess at each end. Turn quilt over and fold end in even with previous finished edge as shown in Figure 25.

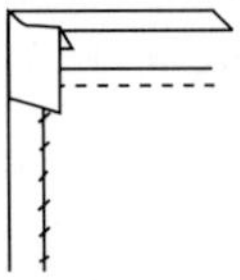

**Figure 25**
Fold end of binding even with previous edge.

Fold binding in toward quilt and stitch down as before, enclosing the previous bound edge in the seam as shown in Figure 26. It may be necessary to trim the folded-down section to reduce bulk.

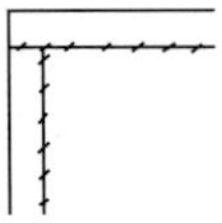

**Figure 26**
An overlapped corner is not quite as neat as a mitered corner.

## Making Continuous Bias Binding

Instead of cutting individual bias strips and sewing them together, you may make continuous bias binding.

Cut a square 18" x 18" from chosen binding fabric. Cut the square once on the diagonal to make two triangles as shown in Figure 27. With right sides together, sew the two triangles together with a 1/4" seam allowance as shown in Figure 28; press seam open to reduce bulk.

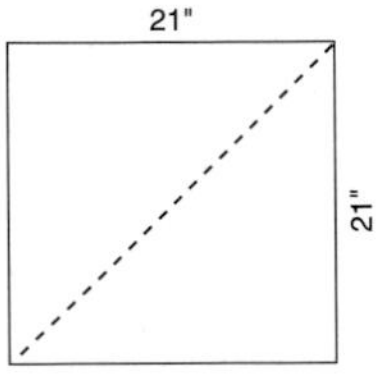

Mark lines every 2 1/4" on the wrong side of the fabric as

**Figure 27**
Cut 21" square on the diagonal.

21"

21"

shown in Figure 29. Bring the short ends together, right sides together, offsetting one line as shown in Figure 30 to make a tube; stitch. This will seem awkward.

Begin cutting at point A as shown in Figure 31; continue cutting along marked line to make one continuous strip. Fold strip in half along length with wrong sides together; press. Sew to quilt edges as instructed previously for bias binding.

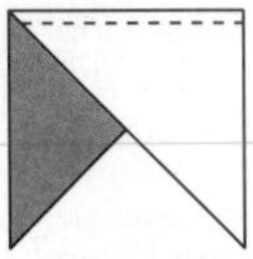

**Figure 28**
Sew the triangles together.

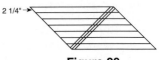

2 1/4"

**Figure 29**
Mark lines every 2 1/4".

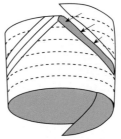

**Figure 30**
Sew short ends together, offsetting lines to make a tube.

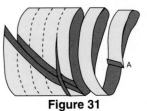

**Figure 31**
Cut along marked lines, starting at A.

## Final Touches

If your quilt will be hung on the wall, a hanging sleeve is required. Other options include purchased plastic rings or fabric tabs. The best choice is a fabric sleeve, which will evenly distribute the weight of the quilt across the top edge, rather than at selected spots where tabs or rings are stitched, keep the quilt hanging straight and not damage the batting.

To make a sleeve, measure across the top of the finished quilt. Cut an 8"-wide piece of muslin equal to that length—you may need to seam several muslin strips together to make the required length.

Fold in 1/4" on each end of the muslin strip and press. Fold again and stitch to hold. Fold the muslin strip lengthwise with right sides together. Sew along the long side to make a tube. Turn the tube right side out; press with seam at bottom or centered on the back.

Hand-stitch the tube along the top of the quilt and the bottom of the tube to the quilt back making sure the quilt lies flat. Stitches should not go through to the front of the quilt and don't need to be too close together as shown in Figure 32.

Slip a wooden dowel or long curtain rod through the sleeve to hang.

When the quilt is finally complete, it should be signed and dated. Use a permanent pen on the back of the quilt. Other methods include cross-stitching your name and date on the front or back or making a permanent label which may be stitched to the back.

**Figure 32**
Sew a sleeve to the top
back of the quilt.

# Fabrics and Supplies

# Special Thanks

*We would like to thank the talented quilt designers whose works are featured in this collection.*

*Vicki Blizzard*
  Ladybugs in the Nine-Patch, 135

*Kathy Brown*
  Bear & 'Coons Bibs, 39
  Around the Block, 96
  Home Is Where the Heart Is, 98

*Pat Campbell*
  Wintry Log Cabin Lattice, 53

*Holly Daniels*
  Sing a Song of Christmas, 50
  Frosty Stars Lap Quilt, 100

*Sue Harvey*
  Rose Garden, 141
  Wisteria Stars, 147
  Prairie Pansies,154

*Sandra Hatch*
  Campfire Nine-Patch, 132
  Purple Fancy, 151

*Connie Kaufmann*
  Monarch Butterfly Pillow, 28

*Pearl Krush*
  Star of the West, 90

*Kate Laucomer*
  Foundation-Pieced Fan Hot Pad, 21
  Spring Flowers Coaster Set, 26
  Happy Holly Table Topper, 56
  Patchwork Pine Trees & Stars, 58
  I'm a Little Angel Sweatshirt, 65
  Angel Messenger, 68

*Joyce Livingston*
  A Touch of Patchwork, 93

*Janice Loewenthal*
  My Dog is an Angel Sweatshirt, 11
  Jolly Santa Tree Skirt, 60
  Happy Holiday Mother/Daughter
      Cardigan, 46
  Blessed Are the Piecemakers, 114
  Clowning Around Kid's Quilt, 159

*Chris Malone*
  Paper-Pieced Gifts, 78
  Melt-Your-Heart Snowman Card Holder, 84

*Karen Neary*
  Festive Holly Place Mats & Napkin Rings, 75

*Jill Reber*
  Quilter's Cosmetic & Sewing Bags, 8
  The Sun, the Moon & the Stars, 103
  Forever Patriotic, 109

*Judith Sandstrom*
  Lovely Lotus Tote, 14
  Choir of Angels, 72
  We Three Kings, 82
  Garden Stars, 124
  Garden Pathways, 138
  Sunflower Patch, 144
  Tilted Star , 157

*Carla Schwab*
  Tasseled Sofa Throw, 24
  Circle of Leaves, 118

*Marian Shenk*
  Sunflower Centerpiece, 18
  Winter Snowflake Sweatshirt, 26
  Baby Bear Sweatshirt, 36
  Sunbonnet Sue, 121
  Table Tulips, 126